Make Your Life Worthwhile

Make Your Life Worthwhile

by
RICHARD ARMSTRONG

TRIDENT PRESS
New York

SBN: 671-27069-9.
Library of Congress Catalog Card Number: 76-124598

Published simultaneously in the United States and Canada
by Trident Press, a division of Simon & Schuster, Inc., 630
Fifth Avenue, New York, N.Y. 10020

Printed in the United States of America

Nihil obstat: Daniel V. Flynn, J.C.D.

Imprimatur: Joseph P. O'Brien, S.T.D., Vicar General, Archdiocese
of New York

Aim—The simple objective is to remind millions of what each person can do to improve the great spheres of influence that shape the destiny of everyone, especially 1) government, 2) education, 3) labor relations, 4) literature, and 5) entertainment.

In God's plan every person has a part to play in applying divine truth to the running of human affairs.

The Name "Christopher"—It comes from the Greek word "Christophoros" meaning "Christ-bearer."

Build Up, Don't Tear Down—The motto of the Christophers is "Better to light one candle than to curse the darkness." God blesses any positive effort to right what is wrong . . . "Be not overcome by evil, but overcome evil with good." (Romans 12:21)

Decide for Yourself—To focus attention on personal responsibility, the Christophers have no organization, no chapters, no memberships, no meetings, no emblems.

How the Idea Is Spread—People in every walk of life are encouraged by the following means to show personal responsibility:

1. *Christopher News Notes* are sent without charge to any adult upon request. They are mailed 7 times a year to 1¼ million persons.
2. The Christopher column appears in 72 daily newspapers.
3. Christopher programs are scheduled daily or weekly on 230 television stations and 2800 radio stations.

Who Pays the Bills?—We depend entirely on voluntary contributions to meet an $800,000 annual budget. . . . All gifts are tax-deductible. (The legal title for wills is: *"The Christophers, Inc."*)

The Christophers
Father Richard Armstrong, M.M., Director
12 E. 48th St., N.Y., N.Y. 10017

Stop and think why it is important to set aside a few still moments each day when you can renew your contact with God and with your own inner self.

With so much to do, so many pressing problems, the individual who seeks to change the world for the better often begrudges even the briefest period of inactivity. Reflecting on eternal truths does not seem to have the urgency of combating poverty, ignorance, discrimination or crime. Thinking about the basic principles that underlie our political or educational systems lacks the excitement of working for good government and schools on the local, state and national levels.

Nevertheless, action in any crucial area of public and private life—if it is to be constructive and effective—must flow from a sure grasp of divine and human values. Its success presupposes a clearly thought-out plan and a constantly purified motivation. That's why each of us needs at least a brief period each day to "come apart and rest a while."

This book starts with familiar, everyday anecdotes—one for each day in the year. It seeks to draw from them their spiritual meaning, to show that even the most routine event in the most ordinary life can be charged with great potential for good or evil.

The implication is clear: it's your life. What you make of it depends, with God's help, on you.

—JAMES KELLER

Make Your Life Worthwhile

The Wonders of Love

There's love in a plastic heart, according to heart surgeon, Dr. Michael DeBakey, of Houston, Texas.

Linda Griggs, 7, of Pittsburgh, sent this question to Doctor DeBakey: "Does a plastic heart have love in it?"

In his reply the doctor wrote: "Yes, a plastic heart does have love in it, a very great deal of love. The love in a plastic heart is the love of many people who love other people, and don't want them to die.

"So these people work all day and often all night to build a heart that will make people live longer." He added: "If you can think of how much love there would be in hundreds of hearts, then that is how much love there is in a plastic heart."

Then he concluded: "When you grow up, you will understand how very much love that is."

There will always be hope for the world so long as person after person, powered by love of God, seeks opportunities to be of service to mankind. Countless ways are open to every one of us.

❖

"Let us love one another; for love is of God."
[1 JOHN 4:7]

❖

Fill our hearts with Your love, O Master, so that we may be more effective in helping others.

Worldwide Mail Delivery by Satellite

A letter mailed in Bombay could arrive in New York in a matter of minutes when an orbiting satellite is used as a post office.

This "instant" worldwide delivery system may be available sooner than we think, according to reports from the Atomic Energy Commission.

Another project will be an orbital newsletter, bringing news from all parts of the world at any time of the day or night.

Moreover, global conference facilities may eventually make international business meetings as common as local telephone calls are today.

The advent of communications satellites should make these exciting discoveries come about within a fairly short time.

Lightning speeds of communication are more and more at the disposal of mankind. It becomes increasingly important, then, that the ideas being transmitted contribute to, rather than detract from, the divinely intended development of all men.

✧

"Be imitators of God, as beloved children. And walk in love, as Christ loved us."

[EPHESIANS 5:1]

✧

Lord, may we use Your creation for the benefit of everyone.

Her Last Good Deed

A 67-year-old woman died as she was helping to bring new life into the world.

Shortly after midnight, she heard the cries of a Brooklyn neighbor who was giving birth.

The elderly woman, active in church and civic affairs, was always ready to extend a helping hand to those in need. She wasted no time in running upstairs to offer assistance.

She succeeded in calming the expectant mother and seemed to have the situation under control. But the strain was too much. She collapsed and died.

To live a life of service involves inconvenience, suffering and in some instances, the sacrifice of one's own life. But to live—and even to die—in such a way is in itself no small accomplishment.

Never forget that the Lord Who made you in His divine image loves you as His child and expects you to return that love, not only to Him but to as many as you can reach during your pilgrimage to heaven.

✣

"He who loses his life for My sake will find it."
[MATTHEW 10:39]

✣

Let me spend my life in doing good to others,
O divine Savior.

Learn and Keep Learning

A famous astronomer was amused by the remark of a 15-year-old girl who sat next to him at dinner.

With youthful candor, she spontaneously asked: "What do you do for a living?"

"I study astronomy," the scientist replied.

"Really?" gasped the wide-eyed teenager. "I finished astronomy last year!"

A person who is deeply in love with truth continues to explore and further his understanding of it all through his life. He is never satisfied with only the beginnings of knowledge.

Whether you are young or old, you will add a plus value to your life if you can say with the great artist Michelangelo: "I am still learning."

See in every person and circumstance a valuable opportunity to deepen and broaden your knowledge. If you do, you will grow in the understanding and wisdom that will help you to become a more effective instrument of divine truth.

✧

"If anyone imagines that he knows something,
he does not yet know as he ought to know."
[1 CORINTHIANS 8:2]

✧

Instill in me, O Holy Spirit, a love for truth.

A Man of Many Talents

A sign reading "Jack of All Trades and Master of Some" decorates an ancient vintage car as its owner drives around St. Louis looking for customers.

He offers services from house wiring and roofing to lessons in drawing, painting and sculpture, according to signs displayed all over his car.

His mobile advertising also includes the following information: "Player pianos repaired, oil paintings cleaned, antique restoration, carpentry, masonry, repairs to automobiles, musical instruments, power mowers and electric appliances."

If you wish to render a real service to others in their problems, small or large, you would do well, with God's help, to develop your own latent abilities.

Good will is necessary to be sure. But much more is required if you wish to make a lasting contribution.

You can leave the world better than you found it if, through competence, skill and hard work, you translate your high ideals into practical action.

✧

"Through love be servants of one another."
[GALATIANS 5:13]

✧

Grant, O Holy Spirit, that I may have both the desire and the ability to change the world for the better.

Telephoning to God

A prankish Londoner picked up his telephone and dialed the letter combination G-O-D. To his surprise a voice replied, "Can I help you?"

Seeking an explanation from the telephone company, he was told that the letters he had dialed were the same numerical combination as Information—I-N-F.

It isn't often that "a call on God" has such an audible answer. Dr. John Haynes Holmes wrote in an article on prayer:

"We go hopelessly astray if we think of prayer as a selfish endeavor to persuade or inveigle, or browbeat God to do us a favor, or win us a victory, or even help us in some dire distress. He is not some kind of divine bellhop, to be summoned by the pressing of a button to the service of our pressing whims. God does not come to us, but we to Him—and prayer is the high road to His presence."

Turn frequently to the Lord as a loving Father Who has your best interests at heart, both for time and for eternity.

❖

"Every one who asks receives, and he who seeks finds, and to him who knocks it will be opened." [LUKE 11:10]

❖

Teach me how to pray, O divine Master.

Procrastination: The Thief of Time

Benjamin Franklin once said "As I grow in years, I find I grow more apt to procrastinate."

The derivation of the word "procrastinate" tells its own story. It comes from "pro" meaning "for" and "cras" signifying "tomorrow."

In defining "procrastinate" the dictionary states that it means "to put off till tomorrow or till a future time; to delay from time to time."

Much good is left undone by persons who habitually postpone duties that should be fulfilled at once.

You owe it to God, as well as to yourself and others, to meet your share of responsibilities promptly and generously.

Failure to do so can cause more than a little harm to your own character, quite apart from shortchanging those who have a right to depend on your immediate cooperation at home, on the job, in civic affairs or in any organization.

"Never put off till tomorrow what you can do today" is an old adage that all of us should keep in mind.

✧

"You know what hour it is, how it is full time now for you to wake from sleep."
[ROMANS 13:11]

✧

Teach me, O Lord, to face responsibilities, not evade them.

17

Young and Old Fulfill One Another's Needs

A unique project called "Foster Grandparents" is giving new hope to 2 groups of people—young children in institutions, and lonely men and women over 60.

The experiment is now being put to work at 5 New York institutions for foundlings and orphans. Qualified men and women are given a 2-week course in the needs of neglected children. The "foster grandparents" are then entrusted with a child of their own to visit 5 days a week.

The director made this comment on the success of the project thus far: "No child can grow and function in a healthy way in society without being helped by a loving, aware adult. And a society filled with hopeless older people is in trouble."

It is heartening to reflect that the Lord made each of us in such a way that our keenest satisfactions are those that arise from trying to fulfill the needs of our fellow human beings.

Find ways to liven your own existence by concerning yourself with other persons.

✧

"Bring the homeless poor into your house."
[ISAIAH 58:7]

✧

Help me, Lord, to involve myself in meeting the wants of others in as selfless a way as possible.

Orbiting Factory Projected in 1990s

A gigantic factory-in-the-sky, housing 328 workers and 72 crewmen, has been proposed by space engineers for the mid-1990s.

As a preparation, a smaller 32-man version would be launched in the early 1980s.

The orbiting factory could be used to discover industrial processes which are possible only in an airless, weightless space environment, or which would greatly profit by it.

These developments might include vacuum refining of metals, cold welding, production of metals and germ-free production of drugs.

In addition the satellite could be used to spot fishing areas, water sources and diseased crops.

Scientific ingenuity is making possible amazing advantages for mankind.

But man must take care that his phenomenal progress in the physical world is matched by a moral and spiritual development that befits a child of God in a space age.

✧

"Be zealous to be found by Him without spot or blemish, and at peace."   [2 PETER 3:14]

✧

Help us, O Father, to use the blessings of Your creation in a truly human way.

Blind Lawyer Has Busy Practice

A lawyer who is known as "the man with the dog" has the distinction of being one of the few totally blind criminal attorneys in the U.S.

This 40-year-old Brooklyn man is always accompanied by a German shepherd dog and it helps his practice.

People just ask for "the man with the dog," he explains, and "someone sends them to me."

It was not until some years after losing his sight that this determined man studied law and passed the bar.

Recalling his first reaction to being without sight, he said: "You are terrified, confused, despondent. But in no time at all you find that living in this new world is an adventure, a day-to-day challenge, exciting to meet."

Man's inexhaustible ability to turn defeat into victory is a tribute to the powers of mind, heart and soul given him by his Creator.

The Lord will bless you if, like this lawyer, you not only overcome setbacks but help others as well.

✧

"I will all the more gladly boast of my weaknesses, that the power of Christ may rest upon me." [2 CORINTHIANS 12:9]

✧

Assist me in conquering discouragement, O Lord, by letting me know how much depends on my efforts.

Much to Learn from the Fly

Scientists are studying flies' eyes in order to learn more about how the human nervous system works.

They also hope to determine how light received by the eye is translated into consciousness and action. Ultimately the research could help in the development of electronic eyes that read print.

"We've been studying many creatures, but the fly seems to fit our needs best," said Dr. Gilbert McCann of the California Institute of Technology in Pasadena. "The fly's nervous system has many properties that are similar to the human system."

Then he added: "The fly can produce enormous amounts of energy for long periods of time on little amounts of nourishment. A healthy fly can make it all the way to San Diego, about 100 miles, in three hours."

Mankind still has much to learn from the magnificent design and the extraordinary efficiency of God's creation. All of nature reflects the wisdom and glory of the Lord's bounty which in His love for all His children He has put at our disposal.

✧

*"Creation waits with eager longing for the re-
vealing of the sons of God."*   [ROMANS 8:19]

✧

Thanks to You, O loving Father, for the wonders of Your creation.

Helping in the Himalayas

Two airline stewardesses learned a new concept of service by volunteering to spend a few months without pay at an orphanage high in the Himalaya mountains.

The young women were first questioned to make sure they both had the maturity and skill to adjust to difficult conditions. Then they began their 3-month stint, teaching children in Nepal basic hygiene and distributing medicines to those in need.

"We arrived during a typhoid epidemic and 2 of the children at the orphanage to which we were assigned died while we were there," they said.

"We volunteered because we thought we could help these people," she added. "We definitely plan to go back and see the children. It's important to let them know you still care about them."

The desire to be of service to those in physical or spiritual need is a deep-seated one. It is a divine trait instilled by God in every person.

Live a fuller, more meaningful life by sharing your love with mankind as far as you can reach.

✧

"You have been a stronghold to the poor, a stronghold to the needy in his distress."
[ISAIAH 25:4]

✧

For Your sake, O Jesus, let me serve those who need people to care about them.

Commuters Lost in Snow

When a blizzard stalled a suburban train one wintry night, the snow was so deep that some 150 commuters dared not leave the crippled train.

Next morning when the half-frozen passengers were able to emerge from their frigid trap, they were startled to see a signal tower only a stone's throw from the stalled cars.

They indignantly demanded an explanation of why the signal-station attendant had done nothing to make known their plight and summon aid.

When questioned, the attendant said he felt no responsibility for the snow-bound train because the spot where it stopped was outside his jurisdiction. "It's not in my territory," he maintained.

Rather than limit your solicitude for others to the narrowest possible confines, reach out to help as many persons as you can.

Innumerable individuals around you and over the earth feel forsaken in their physical, mental and spiritual problems. They need you—and you need them.

✧

"If one member suffers, all suffer together."
[1 CORINTHIANS 12:26]

✧

Help me to see, O Father, that all men are my brothers because they are Your children.

Child's Severed Arm Restored

A little girl whose arm was completely severed can now use it to wash, feed and dress herself.

When an auto collision with a speeding train near Denver, Colorado, badly injured the 4-year-old, her arm was left lying on the ground. But a state policeman saw the arm and put it in the ambulance, thinking that doctors might be able to do something with it. They did.

Eight surgeons, 3 pediatricians and 2 anesthesiologists spent 6 hours attempting the state's first reimplantation of a severed limb.

Sixteen months later the little girl could move her wrist and elbow and some feeling had returned to her hand. Doctors cautiously stated that the arm was "doing quite well."

Despite the heavy odds against success, the law officer's decision vitally affected the girl's future life. In a similar way, as long as we make the effort, the Lord can bring good out of a critical situation. But He expects us to try wholeheartedly.

✧

"He gave skill to men that He might be glorified . . . By them He heals and takes away pain." [SIRACH 38:6]

✧

Give me a sense of undaunted hope, Father, so that with Your help, I may improve even the worst of situations.

Man Pulling Brakes Ties up Subway

A man who pulled the brake cords in all 10 cars of a temporarily stalled subway train caused untold discomfort and
inconvenience for hundreds of people.

It took 36 minutes before the motorman could inch his way
back through the passenger-packed cars to unlock each set of
emergency brakes.

Meanwhile 8 other express trains were re-routed onto local
tracks and the 2 trains immediately behind had to discharge
passengers at the nearest station.

While comparatively few go to such extremes in willfully
inflicting trouble on their fellow men, even one instance of a
thoughtless "I-don't-care" attitude can cause needless pain
and disruption.

Far from letting things slide, take some positive step today
to do more than what is strictly required for the love of God
and others.

The degree to which you put yourself out for your fellow-
men may mean more for time and eternity than you think.

✧

*"I have become all things to all men, that I
might by all means save some."*
[1 CORINTHIANS 9:22]

✧

Help me to work as hard for the benefit of all
men, O Lord, as some do for their destruction.

Falls 15 Floors, Then Phones Home

A man who fell 15 floors in an elevator shaft not only survived but made 4 phone calls. Then he was taken to the hospital in serious condition.

While repairing a 15th floor elevator door in a New York City building, the 35-year-old maintenance man fell down the open shaft. By grabbing some cables, he broke his fall but landed with frightening impact atop the elevator car at street level.

Although badly injured, the plucky man crawled around the cab and up 2 flights of stairs to a telephone. First he called his wife to assure her he was all right. Then he dialed a fellow employee to ask him to take over his duties. Next he phoned his employer to report the accident. Finally he asked police for help.

Such devotion to one's job and consideration for others is far beyond the call of duty. But this valiant example reminds all of us to live up to our responsibilities to God and our fellow man in the ordinary circumstances of life.

✧

"Let steadfastness have its full effect, that you may be perfect and complete, lacking in nothing." [JAMES 1:4]

✧

Instill in me, O divine Master, a keen sense of duty.

Teens Inspire Hopeful Future

Here are some examples of teenagers' thinking, which should inspire hope for the future. They are among 350,000 compositions written for the N.Y. Chamber of Commerce on "Respect for the Rights of Others."

1. "Man's great fund of scientific knowledge renders him capable of creating a peaceful, thriving world. But attempting to do so without first learning to respect the rights of others would be like building a house upon a rotten foundation—it simply cannot be done."
2. "Respect for one another's rights is not confined merely to personal relationships, but is applied also on a national and international level. One of the requisites for world peace is respect for the rights of others and other nations."

Do all you can to ensure that such sentiments are not merely given lip-service by young people, but are put into concrete practice. If you try, God will enable you to achieve heartening results through them.

❖

"Insist . . . that those who have believed in God may be careful to apply themselves to good deeds." [TITUS 3:8]

❖

Let me multiply my efforts for good, O Lord, by inspiring others to carry principles into action.

Breakthrough Against Hunger

A new strain of rice known as IR-8 is a dramatic break-through in Asia's battle against hunger.

Developed in the Philippines, the new rice produces crops two to three times greater than others. It is the result of intensive research in which 10,000 strains of rice were collected for cross-breeding.

A short, sturdy cross between strains from Indonesia and Taiwan, IR-8 grows well even in poor conditions and in any season. Fertilized, it doubles and triples in yield.

Researchers see it as an important advance in the desperate struggle to fill the rice bowls of the underdeveloped countries, where two-thirds of the world's people are chronically undernourished or hungry.

Dedicated experts in many parts of the world are making a relentless effort to find permanent solutions for world hunger.

Pray that they may succeed in developing the vast untapped food resources that a bountiful Creator has provided for the whole of mankind.

✧

"They shall hunger no more."

[REVELATION 7:16]

✧

Inspire us, Holy Spirit, to do what is needed
to provide all people with sufficient food.

Robber Trio Gets Just Deserts

A one-armed man of 76 proved too much for 3 thieves to handle, they found out to their regret.

The thugs jumped the factory messenger as he made his daily trip to the bank with $150 in cash, plus checks and bank books.

The old man wrestled mightily with his good right arm. Finally, the hoodlums got the money away from him and hopped into a getaway car.

But the messenger jumped quickly to his feet, got a clear look at the license number of the auto and jotted it down.

Then he told police, who traced the number and soon rounded up the amazed and disconcerted trio.

Those who trample on the rights of others are seldom brought to justice so speedily. But eventually justice triumphs, even though it may not be in this life.

You can be a cooperator with God Himself by acting with integrity on all occasions. See to it that advantage is not taken of others, especially those less able to defend themselves.

✧

"If God is for us, who is against us?"
[ROMANS 8:31]

✧

Grant me the strength, O Lord, to take a consistent stand for right and truth.

Close Friendships Are Needed

More may be accomplished by talking over personal difficulties with a good friend than by long sessions in doctors' offices.

"A good talk with a close friend can solve problems, or at least put them in perspective before they become overpowering," said Doctor Joseph Matarazzo, who is head of the medical psychology department of the University of Oregon.

"One of the problems we face today is a scarcity of friends. Almost without exception, when I ask a young person who his best friend is, he can't tell me."

He blamed many mental breakdowns on "the lack of close interpersonal relationships," which had been replaced by "the identification with big, impersonal groups instead of individuals."

Thank God for the blessings of true friendships. Seek to be a good friend to others and be willing to put yourself to inconvenience in order to be of service to persons who are in trouble.

✧

"A faithful friend is a sturdy shelter; he that has found one has found a treasure."

[SIRACH 6:14]

✧

Teach me, O divine Master, to reach out in friendship to those who are friendless.

Don't Feel Sorry for Yourself

A valuable lesson can be learned from these words of a 10-year-old boy in Bismarck, N.D., who was born without arms and legs:

"I know there are some things I cannot do. But I think of all the things I can do and I don't worry so much about the rest of it."

Many persons think that because they can't do everything in coping with the problems of life, they need not do anything. No matter how limited your range of action may be, do what you can.

This applies in a special way to the complicated and growing problems of the modern world.

The following lines by Edward Everett Hale may serve as a reminder:

> "I am only one, but I am one,
>   I can't do everything but I can do something,
>   And what I can do, that I ought to do,
>   And what I ought to do,
>   By the grace of God, I will do."

✧

"I have great confidence in you; I have great pride in you."   [2 CORINTHIANS 7:4]

✧

Remind us, O God, that we are important in Your sight.

Always Yearning for "The Good Old Days"

Two tablets dating back to 2800 B.C. were unearthed in Babylon not long ago. They both commented on the trends of the day.

One read: "Times are not what they used to be."

The other tablet reflected a major concern of many people living 28 centuries ago. Their complaint: "The world must be coming to an end. Children no longer obey their parents and every man wants to write a book."

When tempted to frustration or despair over modern trends, take heart in the fact that since the dawn of history the big problem has been to train human beings, both young and old, to act as responsible persons.

While the Creator provides every man with a built-in tendency to do good and avoid evil, it is a never-ending task to train him to be master of himself.

You can help yourself become a more perfect human being by assisting others to bring out their nobler qualities.

✧

"I would have you wise as to what is good and guileless as to what is evil." [ROMANS 16:19]

✧

Grant me the patience, O divine Savior, to find Your holy image in every person.

Tribute to a Teacher

What is a teacher? Here is one answer from an article written some years ago by Joy Elmer Morgan:

"The teacher is a prophet; he lays the foundations of tomorrow.

"The teacher is an artist; he works with the precious clay of unfolding personality.

"The teacher is a friend; his heart responds to the faith and devotion of his students.

"The teacher is a citizen; he is selected and licensed for the improvement of society.

"The teacher is a pioneer; he is always attempting the impossible and winning out.

"The teacher is a believer; he has abiding faith in the improvability of the human race."

You may have neither the calling nor the qualifications to be a teacher. But you can do something to relieve the never-ending need for better teachers.

Encourage at least one competent young man or woman to dedicate his or her God-given talent to the arduous but rewarding work of the classroom.

✧

"Having gifts that differ according to the grace given to us, let us use them."
[ROMANS 12:6]

✧

Bless all teachers, O Master, and enable them to grow in wisdom and understanding.

New Horizons for Older Persons

A retired mechanic, 63, put in a nutshell one of the advantages of a government program that employs older persons to work with neglected and deprived children.

"It's hard to quit," he said, "when you've worked all your life. I'm more interested in these kids than I ever thought I could be. My wife enjoys hearing me talk about my work and it's making us both happier."

Here are other positive aspects of such activities.

- A major new resource of responsible workers for communities and social agencies is provided.
- Emotionally deprived children are given loving companionship, care and attention.
- Innovation is stimulated in the field of child care and institutional administration.

Leisure time best fulfills the purpose intended for it by the Lord when it is personally enriching and adds joy to the lives of others. We could all do with an occasional check-up on how well we use the time that has been put at our disposal.

✧

"What is the measure of my days; let me know how fleeting my life is!" [PSALM 39:4]

✧

Help me recall, O Father, that the most important moment in life is now. May I use it well.

Firemen Perform "Circus" Rescue

Two firemen staged a daring rescue by boldly improvising a trapeze act in a flaming building five stories above a New York City sidewalk.

Thwarted by the dead weight of the victim he was carrying, fireman Bernard Lally couldn't climb to the roof. Flames barred exit to the lower floors.

The other fireman, Lawrence Sloan, gestured with outstretched arms from the roof of a nearby building. But the 4-foot gap was too wide to pass his semi-conscious burden. Lally drew back, then pitched her bodily across the space between the buildings.

For an agonizing instant the 76-year-old woman was unsupported high above the ground. Then Sloan caught her by the shoulders and pulled her to safety.

The greatness that God has instilled in every human being is discovered and translated into action often under the most difficult circumstances.

We can unlock our untapped power for good by being on the lookout for opportunities to be of service to persons in trouble.

✧

"So then, as we have opportunity, let us do good to all men."   [GALATIANS 6:10]

✧

Grant, Lord, that I may be alert to the needs of others.

Plenty of Trouble on Hospital Visit

A man ended up with a broken leg and collarbone, a heart attack and a ruptured stomach after going into a hospital in Buenos Aires to have a bunion removed.

Fearing the pain that might result from the bunion treatment, the patient requested a general anesthetic. It led to the heart attack. By opening his chest and massaging his heart, doctors were able to revive him. Later he suffered a stomach contraction resulting in a rupture of his stomach.

Then while being carried on a stretcher, the patient tumbled off, broke a leg and collarbone and injured his heart further.

At the end of his ordeal, the unfortunate man had a breathing tube in his throat, a drainage tube in his stomach, a leg in plaster and an arm in a sling.

And the bunion was yet to be removed.

It is hard to believe that so much misfortune could befall one individual. But the unhappy experience may remind us not to take for granted the blessings of good health with which God favors us.

✧

"Health and soundness are better than all gold, and a robust body than countless riches."
[SIRACH 30:15]

✧

Thanks, dear Lord, for the many blessings of body and soul that we enjoy.

Big Surprise for Lost Hunter

A tired, starving hunter emerged from the forest where he had been wandering, dropped his rifle and ran to embrace a stranger who had just entered the clearing from the opposite direction.

"Thank heaven, mister!" he exclaimed. "I've been lost for two days. Am I glad to see you!"

"What are you so glad about," murmured the other man. "I've been lost a week!"

We often look for leadership from those poorly qualified to give it. While it may not be too serious in small matters, there is danger of real tragedy in more important affairs.

Whether it is a question of voting for the right candidate, deciding educational policies, joining an organization or deciding the conduct of one's life, take careful thought before acting.

The Lord who has given us intelligence expects us to use it, not only to protect ourselves and those close to us, but also for the good of others. The world needs more real leaders, not just unthinking followers.

✧

"Can a blind man lead a blind man? Will they not both fall into a pit?" [LUKE 6:39]

✧

Help me, O Lord, to be trustful but not gullible; believing but not credulous.

Accepts Thanks but Not Money

A Dutch policeman refused a reward of $7,000 for saving an American's life during World War II.

The man, who traced his rescuer through a Dutch newspaper, finally met him 26 years later.

The police sergeant had twice taken the fugitive from the Nazis to underground addresses before he was imprisoned for his aid to Jewish refugees.

The grateful American gave him a check for 25,000 guilders ($7,000) to express his thanks. But the policeman refused to accept it with these words:

"What I did was my duty—and I accept your thanks but not your money. You are the only one with words of thanks, but I won't accept your money."

We can be grateful to God that in every age He raises up men to go against the dehumanizing tide and act on the basis of firmly rooted conviction.

Accounts of the heroism of others make the rest of us ask ourselves whether we are acting according to our own deepest beliefs in matters affecting public life. Their accomplishments can embolden us to act.

✧

"Go and do likewise."　　　　[LUKE 10:37]

✧

May I be ready to do Your will, Jesus, when the moment of decision arrives.

One Way to Meet a Deficit

One man decided he could do something to help the city of Memphis, Tenn., solve a deficit of $705,000 that it might face by the end of the fiscal year.

He forwarded a check for $6.60 to the city comptroller, pointing out that if each of the city's approximately 650,000 residents would pay $1.10 apiece, the entire deficit could be wiped out.

He said that $3.30 of his payment would cover the share for his family of three. The balance of the check would take care of the share for another family of three who might not be able to pay for themselves.

As the cost of government—local, state and federal—steadily increases, it is vital that every citizen show reasonable concern for expenses. This includes not only deficits but current and proposed financial outlays for the running of public affairs.

God entrusts to each of us many benefits of freedom. But accompanying every civic right is a responsibility that must be conscientiously met if free government is to survive.

✧

"So speak and so act as those who are to be judged under the law of liberty." [JAMES 2:12]

✧

Teach me, Father, to see the merit of small efforts.

No Complaints about His Face

A second grade teacher didn't know it at the time, but one of her pupils was to attract widespread attention because of an essay he wrote in her class.

"My Face" was the subject the Nashville teacher asked her 7-year-olds to write about.

The following lines of one little boy were put so well that they appeared in newspapers all over the country.

"My face has two brown eyes," they began. "It has a nose and 2 cheeks. And 2 ears and a mouth.

"I like my face. I'm glad that my face is just like it is.

"It is not bad, it is not good, but just right."

Being content with one's endowments, physical or spiritual, is not necessarily to be complacent.

Instead of seeking to be or act like others, each of us would do well to accept what has been given us and use it in a way that will reflect credit on the Creator Who has entrusted it to us. Make the most of your powers and live up to your true potential.

✧

"To one he gave five talents, to another two, to another one, to each according to his ability." [MATTHEW 25:15]

✧

Inspire me to fulfill my mission in life, O Lord, by a realistic use of my talents.

What One Egg Can Do

A hard-boiled egg served a unique purpose in Glasgow, Scotland, recently.

A business man who entertained friends at dinner in a local hotel discovered to his embarrassment that he had left his wallet at home, and also his check book.

When presented with a bill for $38.22, he chose a novel way to pay it. Asking the waiter to bring him a hard-boiled egg, he wrote on it a check for the full amount, payable by his bank, and then signed his name to it.

The "egg check" was subsequently forwarded to the bank, where it was carefully rubber-stamped and then credited to the hotel's account.

Regardless of what method a person chooses to meet his obligations, it is important to do so promptly. Unreasonable delays in paying just debts is to deprive others of what is rightfully theirs.

See in every duty, including bill-paying, an opportunity to honor God, respect yourself and benefit others.

✧

"Owe no one anything except to love one another."　　　　　　　　　[ROMANS 13:2]

✧

May I be alert to every opportunity, O Lord, to show my love for You by fulfilling my responsibilities to others.

37 Alligators—Too Many

The owner of 37 alligators and crocodiles recently lost a 2-year battle to keep them in the basement of his Ontario home.

A supreme court justice ruled in favor of the man's neighbors. They claimed that they had suffered a loss of enjoyment of their homes because the alligators and crocodiles gave off a bad odor.

The defendant fainted in court when he was ordered to pay $1,150 to his neighbors and dispose of his pets.

In more ways than we realize do our actions touch the lives of other people. We should therefore be considerate of the legitimate rights of others while pursuing objectives of our own.

You can add a worthwhile note to your own life and serve those within your range of influence if you cultivate the habit of thinking from the other person's point of view before you speak or act.

To show a reasonable concern for the good of everyone is a divine quality that the Master Himself recommends.

✧

"As you wish that men would do to you, do so to them." [LUKE 6:31]

✧

Remind me to be as solicitous for the best interests of other people as I am for my own, O God.

What—Me, a Leader?

Believe it or not, every one of us has some potential for leadership. The job is to find it, increase it and put it constructively to work.

Questions like these may be helpful:

- Do I realize that countless little challenges at home, on the job, at school or in civic life can have long-range consequences? Or do I brush them off?
- Do I familiarize myself with the great issues confronting our country and our world? Or do I succumb to the "It's none of my business" attitude?
- Am I alert to openings all around me . . . by voting regularly . . . taking an interest in school affairs . . . speaking up at meetings . . . writing thoughtful, constructive letters to newspapers, magazines, radio and TV stations and motion picture companies?
- Am I readying myself now for the future by prayer and wholesome self-restraint? Or do I settle for an easygoing existence, expecting the Lord to work wonders when emergencies arise?

❖

"Lift up your eyes, and see how the fields are already white for harvest."   [JOHN 4:35]

❖

Help me to see an opportunity when it comes, Lord, and not to "muff" it.

43

Big Effort for Small Gain

One motorist paid $250 to fight a speeding ticket that would have cost him $10.

The man had been charged with driving 52 miles an hour in a 40-mile zone in New York State. Friends advised him to plead guilty and pay the fine.

Insisting, however, that he had not been speeding, he hired a lawyer, lost two days' pay and traveled 380 miles to appear in court where a judge took his word and tore up the ticket.

While few people would go to so much time, trouble and expense to be cleared of a speeding charge, this determined man proved what stick-to-itiveness can do.

The persistent person seldom loses, whether his cause is good, bad or indifferent. Those who give up without an effort guarantee defeat for even the noblest cause. They fail God, themselves and everybody else.

Great issues confront all of us today. They involve the destiny of men and nations. Give of your best in fighting for the principle at stake and you will have no regrets.

✧

"But he who endures to the end will be saved." [MATTHEW 24:13]

✧

Give me the vision and wisdom, O Holy Spirit, to fight for the truth.

The Heart of a Pain-Wracked Novelist

The career of Carson McCullers, beloved American novelist, was summed up by one critic at the time of the writer's death as "a vocation of pain."

Much of her art, the critic commented, "seemed to have flowed from her own tortured life."

Before she was 29, Carson McCullers had suffered three strokes which paralyzed her left side. Discouraged, she imagined she could never write again. But gradually, a page a day, she resumed her work.

The ever-present pain intensified in her later years. Her husband committed suicide, and illness made her a virtual cripple.

In a rare mention of her troubles she said: "Sometimes I think God got me mixed up with Job. But Job never cursed God, and neither have I. I carry on."

A spirit of trust in God, not without its mixture of irony and hope, can lead us to "carry on."

The happiness and welfare of others may depend on how well we respond to our call. Easy? No. But possible? Yes.

✧

"He knows the way that I take; when He has tried me, I shall come forth as gold."
[JOB 23:10]

✧

Let us see in each cross, Jesus, an opportunity to share in Your suffering and resurrection.

16 Steps to a Tummy Ache

One lad swallowed 16 marbles before he learned that the hand is quicker than the eye.

The 6-year-old from Chesterfield, England, watched his father do a trick that involved "swallowing" a marble and having it come out behind his ear. Then he decided to give it a whirl himself.

When the first marble failed to appear, he tried swallowing another. This went on until he had gulped down 16 in all—but still no luck.

For obvious reasons, he had a stomachache that night. An X-ray the next day showed 16 reasons why.

"When I showed the trick to our 4 children, I never thought any of them would try to do it," his father said, "or I would have explained that I just pretended to swallow the marbles."

Young people tend to be so easily impressed that care is needed lest they be unwittingly misled.

Take no chances about remarks that may give youngsters a wrong direction. The Lord will bless your efforts to avoid needless difficulty for them.

✧

"As you did it to one of the least of these My brethren, you did it to Me."

[MATTHEW 25:40]

✧

Grant me the good sense, O Jesus, not to deceive others, even in jest.

46

Whether You Talk or Not

Most people talk only 10 or 11 minutes a day, according to a survey made by Temple University Medical Center.

Carefully measured tests revealed that the standard spoken sentence takes only 2½ seconds.

The survey pointed out that people do far more communicating with their eyes and eyebrows, facial expressions, hands and shoulders than they do through the spoken word. Silence also conveys one's feelings.

We all communicate our ideas by words, gestures or without making the slightest sounds.

Be sure, then, that the thoughts or impressions that you convey actually reflect the best in you.

Go one step further. See in each remark you make and in every other form of communication an opportunity to share your good ideas with others.

Show your gratitude to God for whatever blessing He has bestowed on you by being His instrument of truth, goodness and beauty.

❖

"I will speak noble things, and from my lips will come what is right."   [PROVERBS 8:6]

❖

Grant me the grace, O Holy Spirit, to know when to speak and when not to.

Every Problem Can Be an Opportunity

An ancient Egyptian chronicler gave this gloomy picture of conditions 4,000 years ago.

"Robbers abound . . . No one plows the land . . . Dirt prevails everywhere . . . The country is spinning round and round like a potter's wheel . . . No longer do we hear anyone laugh . . . The masses are like timid sheep without a shepherd . . . The few slay the many . . . Impudence is rife . . ."

Many people are understandably troubled by similar but far more complicated problems today.

Rather than merely bemoan dangerous trends, take whatever steps you can to treat every problem as an opportunity.

Despite inherent weaknesses, everyone by his God-given nature yearns to do good and avoid evil. The voice of conscience sounds in the depths of every heart. It can be ignored but never completely stifled.

You can give testimony to your divine sense of hope which the New Testament describes as *"a sure and steadfast anchor of the soul."*   [HEBREWS 6:18]

Help me realize, O Lord of history, that every
age had its problems and that we, aided by
Your power, can overcome them.

If You Were Really Poor

What does it mean to live on from $50 to $200 per year? In his book, *The Great Ascent*, Robert L. Heilbroner points out that a family with an income of $6000–$7000 per year would have to:

1. Take out the furniture, except for a kitchen table, a chair and a few old blankets . . .
2. Empty the refrigerator and pantry, except for a small bag of flour, some sugar and salt . . .
3. Take away all the clothing, except for the oldest dress or suit for each member of the family and a shirt or blouse . . .
4. Dismantle the bathroom, shut off the water, remove the electric wiring . . .
5. Cancel all subscriptions to newspapers, magazines and book clubs . . .
6. Throw out the bankbooks and insurance policies and leave the family a cash hoard of $5.

Show appreciation to God for your blessings by making every effort possible to raise the standard of living for the millions stricken by extreme poverty.

✧

"He who has two coats, let him share with him who has none; and he who has food, let him do likewise." [LUKE 3:11]

✧

Teach us, O Father of all, how to be practically concerned with the basic needs of mankind.

49

Cab Driver Proves His Honesty

A taxi driver was handed a $100 bill by mistake by two French women visiting New York City.

The fare for their short trip was less than $1. When the women got out at a busy intersection, one of them gave the cabbie what he thought was a $1 bill—and apparently she did too.

After pocketing it, giving change and receiving a 25 cent tip, the driver went off in search of new fares. Later, when he was making change for another customer, he discovered the mistake.

Going straight to the nearest police station, the cab driver turned the $100 bill over to the officials, expressing the hope "that those two women get their money back."

No matter how widespread dishonesty, cheating, fraud and corruption may be, it is always within the power of every person, thank God, to take a stand for truth and integrity.

Do your part to build an honest world, and everyone will be indebted to you.

✧

"For this I was born, and for this I have come into the world, to bear witness to the truth."
[JOHN 18:37]

✧

May I show by word and deed, Lord, that I am trustworthy.

Man, 89, Teaches Oldsters

An 89-year-old man teaches a class in health and physical education at the Jewish Community Center in St. Louis.

The teacher, Nathan Shatz, is a retired dress designer. He lives by what he calls "six ingredients for life"—correct breathing, a balanced diet, plenty of water, exercise, cleanliness, and sunshine.

All the men in Mr. Shatz' class are 60 or older. He expressed his happiness in having the opportunity to teach them to enjoy healthier, longer lives.

No matter what our age, it is important that we seek practical ways of serving the best interests of our fellow men.

But for persons advanced in years, it is particularly beneficial and stimulating to them to act as agents of the Lord by contributing to the well-being of everybody.

By sharing with others what they treasure themselves, they add a new dimension to their own lives.

✧

"Let days speak, and many years teach wisdom." [JOB 32:7]

✧

Let me learn, Lord, to find my happiness in making other people happy.

Good Writing Helps Everybody

An expert in written communications at the University of Paris, Prof. Cyrille Arnavon, gives the following pointers for developing fledgling writers:

- Master a good vocabulary. Use your dictionary.
- Know how to use words. Vocabulary is not enough.
- Develop your own style. No two are alike.
- Organize facts, but leave something to inspiration.
- Begin with a brief, telling statement.
- Learn to shift easily from one idea to another.
- Pause, after half a dozen sentences, or a page.

Check what you have written for clarity, logic, consistency, aptness of phrase and idiom. Consider its appeal to readers.

Important as technique may be, the writer must be something himself before he can convey anything of value to others.

If you have the desire to communicate, based on a Christ-like love for people, you will be more likely to add force, clarity and motivation to everything you write.

❖

"Out of the abundance of the heart, the mouth speaks." [MATTHEW 12:34]

❖

Stir in me, Lord, a sincere wish to put good ideas across, and a willingness to listen to others.

Thy Will Be Done

A friend of Abraham Lincoln tried to console him in his many presidential problems by saying one day: "I hope that the Lord is on our side."

To everyone's amazement, Lincoln replied kindly but emphatically that this was not his hope.

Then he went on to say: "I am not at all concerned about that, for we know that the Lord is always on the side of the right. But it is my constant anxiety and prayer that I and this nation should be on the Lord's side."

The problem is not a question of God fitting into our plans, because the very reason for our existence is to accommodate ourselves to His plans.

The big job to be done, especially in our day, is to fulfill that portion of the Lord's prayer that says: "Thy will be done on earth as it is in heaven."

We can all help to bring the peace and order of heaven to this troubled world.

✧

"Shine as lights in the world, holding fast the word of life."   [PHILIPPIANS 2:15]

✧

Help me, O Lord, to play a part in bringing Your peace upon earth.

Lens Found by Sifting Snow

A resourceful mother in Grand Rapids, Mich., refused to be discouraged when her 17-year-old son lost one of his expensive contact lenses in a snowbank.

Acting under her instructions, he shoveled the snow into buckets, melted it and poured the water through a sieve. In a half hour they found the lens.

In our complex and often perplexing age, a little hope, determination and prudent action can spell the difference between victory and defeat.

Grumbling solves nothing and may even make a bad situation worse.

Once you appraise the "ins and outs" of a problem, whether on the local scene or in the larger world, get beyond self-pity by doing something, however small, to improve it.

Each of us, with the help of God, can play a part in rediscovering lost values and applying them in a way that will turn liabilities into assets.

You may surprise yourself by the results to be gained from a hopeful "can do" attitude.

❖

"I will hope continually, and will praise You yet more and more."　　[PSALM 71:14]

❖

Give me the strength, O Lord, to overcome discouragement and strive to bring good out of evil.

Love Should Be "Always"

In 1925 Irving Berlin published the song "Always." It has been popular ever since.

Its basic theme is that love should be distinguished by sincerity and understanding that is for "always."

The closing refrain of the song accentuates the idea that love should be permanent and timeless—that it should be "not for just an hour, not for just a day, not for just a year, but ALWAYS."

While practically everyone wishes to be loved endlessly, too few of us in turn show a willingness to love our fellow men in fair weather and foul, through thick and thin—forever.

In attempting to perfect our love for others and make it more enduring, we would do well to imitate the "always" love that the Creator Himself has for each of us.

No matter how changeable and inconstant we may be, the Lord is a loving Father to us always. He expects us to care for one another with the same lasting love with which He loves us.

✧

"*I have loved you with an everlasting love.*"
[JEREMIAH 31:3]

✧

Grant, O Lord, that I love others with the same constancy with which You love me.

Rules for Quitting Job

Dissatisfied with your job? Before you do anything about it, consider points like these:

1. Ask yourself whether you have given your present assignment the best that is in you. If not, you are cheating both your boss and yourself.
2. Seek advice from friends who can give you an objective appraisal of your situation.
3. Make sure that any change you make is for the better. This involves not only personal satisfaction but also the contribution you can make to the good of others.
4. Prepare for your next position. This may require some further study or training.
5. Do not quit in anger. Most people experience temporary setbacks and frustrations. A weighty decision should be preceded by calm reflection.
6. Leave your employer and co-workers with pleasant memories about you.
7. Pray for divine guidance in distinguishing between a laudable desire to excel and a move dictated by pride, pique or novelty.

✧

"Commit your work to the Lord, and your plans will be established." [PROVERBS 16:3]

✧

Let me know Your Will, O Father, and not hesitate to carry it out.

They Met with a Bang

A new chapter of the ageless "boy meets girl" story was written not long ago in Oslo, Norway.

It began when a motorist struck a young woman at a busy street corner. He wasted no time in rushing her to the hospital.

During her recovery, he became a regular visitor. Later, he asked her to marry him and she agreed. They took their honeymoon in the car that caused the accident.

However varied or amusing may be the ways in which married couples first meet, the most important chapter of their life opens after they say "I do."

Bring home especially to those who are contemplating marriage the weighty life-long obligations involved as well as the joys.

The Lord will bless any and every effort you make to spread far and wide the true meaning of marriage.

If you do, there is no telling how many persons you will help to deepen and intensify their love as the years roll on.

❖

"So they are no longer two but one. What therefore God has joined together, let not man put asunder." [MARK 10:9]

❖

Help me, O Lord, to strengthen the ties of family life in every way I can.

Don't Overlook the Need for Perseverance

Fritz Kreisler was approached backstage by an enthusiastic music fan who cried: "Mr. Kreisler, I'd give my life to play as you do!"

Quietly he replied: "Madam, I did."

Achievement requires sacrifice. Nobody knows this better than the dedicated father or mother. Likewise the devoted artist, the struggling writer and the selfless public servant all pay a price for whatever they may accomplish. Long hours, loneliness and frustration are part of the game. But it's worth the effort!

Your children will have to come to grips with a complex and challenging world.

Teach them to treat all people with respect . . . Encourage their God-given idealism . . . Praise their efforts on behalf of others . . . Place a value on healthy competition . . . Point out that new ideas are rooted in honored traditions of the past.

Help them to keep up with a changing world and change it for the better.

✧

"By your endurance you will gain your lives."
[LUKE 21:19]

✧

Never permit me to lose perseverance, Lord,
in striving for worthwhile goals.

Unusual Generosity for Fire Victims

A kind-hearted bus line employee gave away his apartment to a homeless family in New York City when a blaze destroyed their home and belongings.

Hearing from a social worker friend of the family's plight, the 26-year-old Greyhound Lines employee did what came "automatically"—he offered his own apartment to the stranded family.

"They had no place to stay, and no clothes," he commented. "I have seen a lot of cases of this sort and just felt it was my turn to do a good turn. I just wanted to do my part like anybody else."

As for his own plans, he said: "I guess I'll room with a friend for the time being."

The refreshing part of this man's action is the matter-of-fact way in which he put himself to great inconvenience for a family he didn't even know.

The brotherhood of man under God's fatherly care provides solid promise of a peaceful future. If enough individuals can be motivated to share with those in need, there is hope for the world.

✧

"He who loves his brother abides in the light."
[1 JOHN 2:10]

✧

Never let me close my eyes or my heart to a person in need, Lord, for You have made us all brothers.

Old Bible Saved from Destruction

Several rare books—which were almost thrown away over 40 years ago—were discovered recently at Baker University in Kansas.

The volumes were found in a storeroom in a dusty old box together with other books marked for discard. For some reason, the box was never disposed of.

One of them was an original copy of the Somerset Bible, printed in 1813. It was described as the first Bible printed west of the Allegheny Mountains.

Another was a Bible published by Noah Webster in 1833. The third was an 18th century Methodist hymnal published in London.

It is always cause for gratitude that an ancient book, especially the Bible, is rescued from oblivion. But whether in a new edition or old, keep in mind that in the Holy Bible God speaks to you in the living present.

Set aside a few minutes daily to read and reflect prayerfully upon a passage from the New or Old Testament. Then apply its teachings to modern life!

✧

"For whatever was written in former days was written for our instruction." [ROMANS 15:4]

✧

Let me find in Your word, O Lord, the strength to fulfill my mission in life.

Strange Diet for Bullfrogs

Feeding potato chips to bullfrogs made the difference between success and failure for a Chinese farmer on the island of Formosa.

Cheng Chiun had one of the 70 breeding farms for frogs that were imported from Japan in 1950 in the hope of developing local industry.

Most of the farms failed because they could not find food enough for the frogs. But Mr. Cheng tried the potato chip diet and found it much to their liking.

As they grew older he switched them to a diet of ground fish and snails. Some 40,000 frogs now flourishing on his farm sell for $7.50 a pair.

The enterprising man will usually find a way to come out on top while those with less vision and determination tend to fall by the wayside.

But if prosperity in business can motivate such resourcefulness, how much more should the love of God prod us to find effective solutions to the problems that plague mankind. Use your ability to help solve at least one of these problems.

✧

"Aim at what is honorable not only in the Lord's sight but also in the sight of men."
[2 CORINTHIANS 8:21]

✧

Let me be as zealous, O Jesus, in protecting the rights of others as I am in furthering my own interests.

61

Your Amazing Brain

Your brain is capable of tremendous possibilities. During a lifetime, according to one scientist, it could store about 50 times more information than is contained in the 9 million volumes of the Library of Congress.

A medical expert paid this tribute to the brain: "If all of the equipment of all the telegraphs, telephones, radios and television sets of the North American continent could be squeezed into a half-gallon vase, it would be far less intricate than the three pints of brain that fill your head."

There is little danger of exaggerating the wonders of your brain. With its 12 billion nerve cells or neurons, it is much more than a message center or telephone exchange. It is also an amazing reservoir of energy that stimulates and controls every part of your body.

Show your gratitude to your Creator for the precious gift of your mind by putting it to use as fully and constructively as you can. Help others also to appreciate the blessing of intelligence and to seek opportunities to apply its powers to our fast-changing times.

✧

"Every good endowment and every perfect gift is from above, coming down from the Father of Lights."　　　　　　　　[JAMES 1:17]

✧

Thanks to You, O Lord of lords, for allowing me to share in Your divine intelligence.

Listen to George Washington

When George Washington took the oath of office as first President of the United States on April 30, 1789, he spontaneously added this four-word prayer of his own: "So help me God"—an invocation still used in official oaths by those taking public office, in courts of justice and in other legal proceedings.

In the first part of his Inaugural Address, immediately following the oath, Washington reverently acknowledged our country's dependence on Almighty God:

". . . it would be peculiarly improper to omit in this first official act, my fervent supplications to that Almighty Being who rules over the universe—who presides in the councils of nations—and whose providential aids can supply every human defect, that His benediction may consecrate to the liberties and happiness of the people of the United States, a government instituted by themselves for these essential purposes . . ."

Do your part to protect and deepen the spiritual roots upon which the very survival of freedom depends.

❖

"There exists no authority except from God."
[ROMANS 13:1]

❖

Thanks to You, O Lord of lords, for the precious blessing of freedom.

Businessman Aids Indian Population

Despite "it can't be done" advice from friends, one young businessman in Oklahoma built up a successful enterprise employing poverty-stricken Indians.

When Donald Greve, 34, saw the plight of the jobless Indian population in Andarko, Oklahoma, he decided to start a carpet mill there.

With $150,000 he raised together with 4 associates, plus some government help, he was able to employ 276 Indians on a full-time basis.

The mill provided a profit-sharing plan, free hospitalization, life insurance, free legal counsel and a scholarship plan for employees' families. Non-profit homes for workers were also built.

To provide for the legitimate needs of others in the course of one's ordinary duties is a goal worth striving for.

God has endowed each of us with certain unique abilities of mind, heart and soul. How well we use them in a spirit of loving service will greatly affect ourselves and many others for time and eternity.

✧

"Render justice to the afflicted and the destitute. Rescue the lowly and the poor."

[PSALM 82:3,4]

✧

Inspire me, Lord, not to be deterred by difficulties in seeking ways to benefit others.

Loses Leg and "Finds Life"

A former beauty queen who lost a leg to bone cancer can now say, "I found my life."

The girl was a senior at Oklahoma State University when her left leg was amputated. Now she looks at the ordeal as being, in its own way, a blessing.

"For the first time in my life I had to take stock. I asked myself, 'Who do you want to be? Do you want to die or do you want to live?' "

"I decided I was not going to become a vegetable, and for the first time in my life I was really living," she recalled.

She returned to college for a degree in education, and hopes to help crippled servicemen adjust to life.

"I'll tell them it takes only one leg to climb, if you really want to get somewhere," she said.

People who surmount obstacles have one thing in common: they take a hard look at themselves and concentrate on what they can do instead of lamenting what they cannot. Ask God for the strength to do just that.

✧

"After you have suffered a little while, the God of all grace . . . will Himself restore, establish and strengthen you." [1 PETER 5:10]

✧

Guide my thinking, Lord, into hopeful channels and my actions into constructive ones.

Brakes Fail, but Truck Driver Doesn't

A driver stayed with his runaway truck as it raced downhill and so probably saved the lives of several school-children on their way home to lunch.

The 27-year-old truck driver told police that the brakes on his heavily laden vehicle gave way shortly after he started down a long hill.

Seeing children straggling into the street as he neared the school, the quick-thinking man hopped from the driver's seat onto the running board. Then he shouted warnings to the young people while steering the truck with one hand.

No children were hit but the man himself suffered minor injuries. He was thrown from the speeding truck just before it hit 2 parked cars and came to a stop with one of its wheels broken.

Persons who have the interests of others at heart are usually alert and resourceful in coming to their assistance in times of danger.

Deepen your love for people in all walks of life and you will more effectively develop your own God-given powers.

✧

"I lay down My life for the sheep."
[JOHN 10:15]

✧

Let me learn to live a fuller, richer life, O Savior, by showing a solicitude for others in need.

Show Courage in Your Life

Do you know the origin of the word "courage"? It comes from the Latin word "cor," meaning "heart." The dictionary defines it as "that quality of mind which meets danger or opposition with calmness and firmness."

Here are a few reflections on courage:

> "Courage consists, not in hazarding without fear, but being resolutely minded in a just cause."   [PLUTARCH, 120 A.D.]
>
> "A great deal of talent is lost in this world for the want of a little courage."
>   [SYDNEY SMITH, 1845]
>
> "Often the test of courage is not to die but to live."   [ALFIERI, 1785]

While many admire physical bravery, far more important is moral courage which involves setting one's heart on a right course of action despite disapproval, contempt or opposition.

It may not be easy, but those who labor to share their own spiritual and temporal advantages with others have this divine assurance of Jesus Christ:

✧

> "My peace I give you . . . Let not your hearts be troubled, neither let them be afraid."
>   [JOHN 14:27]

✧

Enlighten me, O Holy Spirit, that I may know what is right and strengthen me to do it.

"Lights Candles" in Prison Work

Teaching in a prison may strike some as depressing. But Richard Burns, 45, who admits the problems, then goes on to add: "But that doesn't stop me from 'lighting one candle, instead of cursing the darkness.' "

Mr. Burns administers the educational program at Maryland Penitentiary. He grew up in the slums of East Baltimore. After a time in the army, he went to Morgan State College on the G.I. Bill, graduating with honors.

Today he teaches many men whom he knew as a child, men who had failed where he had succeeded. But, Mr. Burns says, "It was not the time for me to gloat over my personal success. I felt I had to help them.

"When I see these men armed with the new weapons of knowledge instead of the old weapons of violence and ignorance," he added, "I know that there is new hope for the men and new hope for all of us."

So long as there are individuals who care enough to give of themselves so that others might have a chance, there is, thank God, hope for us all.

✧

"Let your light so shine before men, that they may see your good works and give glory to your Father in heaven." [MATTHEW 5:16]

✧

When I learn of the worthwhile accomplishments of others, Jesus, may it spur me to imitate their spirit.

The Dog Did His Part

A barking puppy tried unsuccessfully to get a message to the man who carried him home from the veterinarian's in Memphis, Tennessee.

When they arrived, the man told his wife about the dog's behavior.

"He didn't enjoy the visit," he told his wife. "He barked all the way home as if he were trying to tell me something."

The wife took a close look at the dog and said: "You're right. He was trying to tell you that you brought the wrong dog home."

It is a human failing to pay little heed to the reminders that God sends each of us from all sides.

Don't disregard the warnings that your own conscience offers or those that come from family, friends, acquaintances —or even from little dogs.

Try to be reasonably alert to every admonition that draws you towards doing what is right and away from drifting into needless mistakes.

✧

"Watch therefore, for you know neither the day nor the hour." [MATTHEW 25:13]

✧

Guide and strengthen me, O Holy Spirit, especially when I wander away from truth.

Spending Has Limits

Bankruptcy faces a fraternal organization in London because it is, by its own admission, living beyond its income.

"We are having to sell our investments to meet day-to-day costs," a representative said. "The plain fact is that we are spending more than we get in contributions—and that's the road to ruin."

Living within one's means is a habit difficult for many to acquire. But no person or organization, business or government can continuously spend more than it has.

It is never too early to learn the importance of balancing income and expenses. Parents could fortify their children for life and avoid many headaches by teaching them the elementary values and practices of budgeting their funds, be they nickels or dollars.

God expects us to show reasonable caution in managing the material goods He entrusts to us. And He urges us to use them for the benefit of others as well as our own.

✧

"Beware of all covetousness; for a man's life does not consist in the abundance of his possessions." [LUKE 12:15]

✧

Thanks to You, O generous Provider, for the material blessings I enjoy.

The Long Hard Fall

A daredevil parachutist safely fell 7,200 feet to the ground—all without benefit of his parachute.

The Texan, a member of a sky-diving club, set out to plummet to about 2,000 feet before pulling the ripcord. At that height he did so but one of the lines fouled.

Then he tried the second chute, but he was spinning so furiously that nothing happened. There was no alternative but to await the inevitable.

By good fortune the man landed in a rice paddy. He had nothing more to show for his mile-plus fall than a not-too-serious back injury.

"Throw a lucky man into the sea," runs an Arab saying, "and he will come up with a fish in his mouth."

While being thankful to God for whatever fortunate circumstance may come our way, we should never let ourselves be tricked into foolhardiness.

Ordinary prudence, whether in driving the family car or in trying to correct an evil situation, is the watchword of the wise man. Avoid deceiving yourself.

✧

"If any one loves righteousness, her labors are virtues; for she teaches self-control and prudence, justice and courage." [WISDOM 8:7]

✧

Keep me from timidity, O Lord, but keep me also from taking unnecessary chances.

Loneliness for Aged Overcome

One answer to a major problem of old age—loneliness—is being met in Vienna. More than 100 clubs have been organized for retired people.

During the fall and winter, they can gather together in comfortable rooms. Newspapers and magazines are at their disposal. But what is prized more than anything else is the companionship of others, with whom they can reminisce or play cards.

They enjoy also the afternoon snack of Viennese coffee and rolls served to everyone.

In addition, the older people are provided with two "carefree days" a month. Twice a month, the clubs arrange things so that they do not have to go shopping, cook or wash the dishes. All these services are done free of charge.

God will bless your smallest effort to make life a bit more interesting for older people.

By showing that you truly care, you can brighten their lives as well as protect them from the pangs of loneliness.

✧

"Do not cast me off in the time of old age;
forsake me not when my strength is spent."
[PSALM 71:9]

✧

Lord, may I show a concern for the problems of older people.

A Light in the Darkness

A fire engine and a group of stranded motorists were all grateful for a tiny lantern that led them to safety in a heavy fog recently.

Things had misted over so badly one night in Lawrence, Mass., that the powerful beams of the fire truck could not penetrate the obscurity.

Then one of the men hopped out of the big vehicle with a hand lamp and guided it step by step along the highway. The motorists in turn were able to inch their way by following the glow from the brightly illuminated fire engine.

In its own way this incident is a reminder of the Christopher motto: "Better to light one candle than to curse the darkness."

The often bewildering darkness of modern problems may at times tempt us to repay evil with evil. But even one constructive prayer, word or deed done for love of Christ can be the start of an incalculable chain reaction for good.

Instead of bewailing evil, light a candle!

✧

"Do not be overcome by evil, but overcome evil with good."   [ROMANS 12:21]

✧

Fill me with the faith and hope, O Lord, to get beyond selfish interests to spread Your love.

Baby Shows Athletic Prowess

Being able to roller-skate at the age of 10 months is no small accomplishment.

But for a little boy from Southern California, it's just part of growing up. The athletic baby was able to stand, much to the astonishment of doctors, when he was 4 days old and could walk with a little help at 2 weeks.

Aloft on his 6-year-old sister's skates one day, he wobbled for about 3 feet into her arms.

"We'll buy him a pair of skates of his own pretty soon," his proud father said, "if he keeps going this way."

It's the rare child that can perform such physical feats at this tender age. But alert parents can often discover and encourage the many hidden facets of their children's personalities.

The Lord has given children to the care of their parents to fit them for life in which each of them has a mission to perform. Train them with kindness and give them a noble goal as they begin their journey to heaven.

✧

"Let the children come to Me." [MARK 10:14]

✧

Enlighten me, O Holy Spirit, so that I may build up, and never dampen, the power of young people.

Hope in Action

Hope looks for the good in people instead of harping on the worst.

- Hope opens doors where despair closes them.
- Hope discovers what can be done instead of grumbling about what cannot.
- Hope draws its power from a deep trust in God and the basic goodness of mankind.
- Hope "lights a candle" instead of "cursing the darkness."
- Hope regards problems, small or large, as opportunities.
- Hope sets big goals and is not frustrated by repeated difficulties or setbacks.
- Hope pushes ahead when it would be easy to quit.
- Hope puts up with modest gains, realizing that "the longest journey starts with one step."
- Hope accepts misunderstandings as the price for serving the greater good of others.
- Hope is a good loser, because it has the divine assurance of final victory.

✦

"Hope does not disappoint us, because God's love has been poured into our hearts."
[ROMANS 5:5]

✦

Fill me with a sense of divine hope, Lord, so that I may push ahead despite difficulties.

How to Think Straight

1. Think for yourself—If you weigh, examine, and sift the evidence, you will be more likely to find the truth and share it with others.
2. Think before you act—Even a moment's reflection may have far-reaching consequences for good.
3. Think objectively—Develop the facility to get beyond a narrow, selfish point of view.
4. Think ahead—Cultivate the habit of looking beyond the present.
5. Think hopefully—A hopeful person sees an opportunity in every calamity while a cynic sees a calamity in every opportunity.
6. Think things through—Much fuzzy thinking could be clarified if more persons would think things through and thus avoid making rash or erroneous judgments.
7. Think charitably—A genuine love for others for love of God is the best preparation for clear, unbiased thinking.
8. Get beyond wishful thinking—Discipline yourself to carry your good thoughts into constructive action.

✧

"A man's mind plans his way, but the Lord directs his steps."   [PROVERBS 16:9]

✧

Help me, O Lord, to think and act at all times with faith, hope and love.

Boomerang Attempt Backfires

The Eiffel Tower is no place to throw a boomerang, one unthinking man found to his regret.

He hurled his curved instrument around the first landing of the 984-foot monument, expecting it to make a full circle and return to him.

Instead, his first throw nearly hit a tourist in the head. He did no better on his second and third attempts.

By this time apprehensive tourists complained to Tower authorities and the unsuccessful boomerang artist was politely told to practice elsewhere.

Legitimate recreation has its place. Our freedom to do so, however, is limited by the consideration: "What will it mean to others?"

If you are looking for moments of relaxation that truly build up instead of tear down, you will take into account more than your own interests.

See God's holy image in every person you meet and you will be far more likely to further the good of everybody, including yourself.

✧

"When God created man, He made him in the likeness of God."   [GENESIS 5:1]

✧

Give me a healthy regard for others, O Jesus, and help me act accordingly.

This Elephant Likes Red Cars

A woman's red station wagon was crushed by an elephant in Vancouver, B.C. The owner of the animal apologized and explained that it had the unfortunate habit of sitting on vehicles of that color.

Her auto was still drivable. But on the way to a garage she was caught up in a traffic jam caused by an automobile accident. Moments later an ambulance arrived. Attendants ran over to assist her.

"Oh, I wasn't involved in this accident," the woman said. "An elephant just sat on my car."

Upon hearing that, both the ambulance crew and policeman decided to rush her to the hospital for possible shock and head injuries.

In confronting the many and varied hazards of modern life, try to meet them with as much calm and conviction as possible under the circumstances.

Deepen your own inner life, especially by prayer and meditation, and you are more likely to control any situation, however perplexing or frustrating, rather than be defeated by it.

✧

"Accept whatever is brought upon you, and in changes that humble you be patient."

[SIRACH 2:4]

✧

Grant, O Lord, that I may trust You in all the vicissitudes of life.

It's Your Government

The man who set 15 garages afire and turned in 15 false alarms in Buffalo, N.Y., gave an odd explanation for his strange behavior.

"I don't like to see firefighters sitting around a fire house doing nothing. They should be working," he told police.

There are many risks in jumping to groundless conclusions regarding the performance of public servants. Everyone involved suffers.

Before you allow yourself to reach a judgment about the seeming shortcomings of any person in government, make sure you base your verdict on fact, not fantasy.

Better still, if you think there are defects in any phase of public service, do something to right what is wrong, rather than take a hostile, negative attitude.

It is your government as much as it is anyone's. Protect your own God-given freedom and that of everyone else by strengthening every weakness you find.

✧

"Let us choose what is right; let us determine among ourselves what is good."   [JOB 34:4]

✧

Thanks, O loving Father, for the precious blessings of liberty. Help me to cherish and protect it.

26 Hours on a Subway

Five college students traversed the subways of New York—
every foot of the 236 miles of track—in 25 hours, 57 minutes.

The collegians worked far in advance to figure out the
quickest route, down to the last transfer, in traveling the
world's longest subway ride—and all of it on one thin token.

The students, members of the Rapid Transit Club of
Massachusetts Institute of Technology, planned their unusual
jaunt to nowhere with a purpose in mind. They had hopes of
duplicating the subway system on a computer and thus helping the underground railway provide better service for its
millions of passengers.

People who are motivated by a desire to serve the best
interests of their fellow men are usually imaginative and
enterprising.

Use the talent God entrusted to you in behalf of others,
not only for your own personal advantage, and you may be
happily surprised at your resourcefulness.

✤

*"I try to please all men in everything I do,
not seeking my own advantage, but that of
many."* [1 CORINTHIANS 10:33]

✤

Grant me the vision, O Lord, to be alert to
the needs of others.

Blind Man Helps Mentally Ill

A blind man—with no hands—serves as rehabilitation counselor for the mentally ill in Illinois.

He tries to help them return to productive, everyday activities.

Twelve years ago, the 27-year-old blind man was like other youngsters. While playing one day with improperly mixed chemicals, they exploded. He lost his sight and both hands.

Despite his handicap, the boy completed high school and learned braille. After college, he acquired a master's degree in vocational rehabilitation.

Praising the resourcefulness of the young man, an official said: "He's bright, he's learning a lot and he's teaching others. He will eventually train six more rehabilitation counselors in the district."

No matter what our limitations, each of us can do something, with God's help, to lighten the burdens of other people. By doing so we can perform a valuable service as well as add something to our own lives.

✧

"Encourage and strengthen him; for he shall go over at the head of this people."
[DEUTERONOMY 3:28]

✧

Let me imitate You, Lord, in reaching out to persons who are afflicted in body or spirit.

Partial Checklist for Marriage Preparation

The immaturity of husbands and wives is one of the most frequent and crushing causes of broken homes.

This is just one reason why teenage boys and girls should start early to get ready for a home of their own.

To be an effective husband and father requires serious preparation.

A young man can do this by showing a sensitivity to the feelings and rights of others. He can also develop habits of thoroughness, decisiveness and reliability in fulfilling his present obligations.

To be a devoted wife and mother likewise involves a preparation that should begin in the early teens.

Besides increasing her capacity for an enduring love of husband and children, a young woman should acquire the skills and qualities of a good homemaker. Among these are cooking, sewing, neatness, order, economy, punctuality, and unending patience.

With such healthy habits and attitudes, based on love of God, the prospects for marital happiness are considerably brighter.

✧

"Let each one of you love his wife as himself, and let the wife see that she respects her husband." [EPHESIANS 5:33]

✧

Inspire me, O Holy Spirit, to give proper guidance to those preparing for marriage.

A *Fireman on Fire*

Discovering a blaze in his own shirt pocket was the surprise that confronted one fireman on his way back to the station house in Kalamazoo, Mich.

When the 33-year-old man smelled smoke very close to him, he investigated and discovered he was on fire himself.

Upon opening his coat, he found the entire front of his shirt was ablaze. The fire was put out before he suffered any injury.

The fireman recalled that when the alarm sounded, he had stuffed his pipe into his shirt pocket and put on his rubber coat, without realizing that the pipe was still smouldering.

You may never find your shirt on fire, but just the same, it would pay to check from time to time to make sure that there are no hidden defects within you that could cause harm to yourself as well as others.

Strive also to improve yourself physically, intellectually and spiritually and you will be better fitted to be of service to others.

✧

*"But who can discern his errors? Clear thou
me from hidden faults."*   [PSALM 19:12]

✧

Help me to look into myself, O Lord, and correct my own shortcomings rather than find fault with others.

Running Away Isn't the Answer

Pulling a vegetable cart got too confusing for one Brooklyn horse so he took off at a fast pace after snapping the straps of his harness.

Loco (his name) was soon pursued by no less than a dozen police cars. The runaway, who raced through red lights and down one-way streets the wrong way, held a considerable advantage over the law-abiding police cars.

Three miles and 25 minutes later, the puffing stallion was cornered in a garage and returned to his owner in good condition.

Most of us get the urge to "jump the traces" at times, when responsibilities begin to weigh us down.

But running away from our duties to God, ourselves or those who depend on us invariably results in greater burdens than those we try to dodge.

Face the duties of your state in life manfully and you can be sure the Lord will do His part to see that you persevere.

✧

"My grace is sufficient for you, for My power is made perfect in weakness."
                                        [2 CORINTHIANS 12:9]

✧

Strengthen my resolve, O Holy Spirit, to cheerfully live up to every challenge that comes along.

Actor's Words Frighten Prowler

A retired Shakespearean actor knew just what to do when he saw someone trying to jimmy the window of his son's house nearby.

Reaching for his sword (a theatrical prop), the 82-year-old man rushed out at the prowler declaiming those chilling words from "Macbeth":

"Avaunt! and quit my sight! Let the earth hide thee! Thy bones are marrowless, thy blood is cold."

This was too much for the would-be thief, who ran away without a fight.

Words can be, in Emerson's phrase, "as hard as cannon-balls," especially when they strike on a guilty conscience.

But in other circumstances, well-chosen words can soothe the distressed, give heart to the downcast or inspire the fearful.

The words we utter can be the cause of much good or harm. Ask God, therefore, for the wisdom to frame your speech so that it will further the happiness of others, not detract from it.

✧

"If anyone makes no mistakes in what he says he is a perfect man."   [JAMES 3:2]

✧

Be in my heart and on my lips, O Lord, that I may use my tongue to Your glory.

One Way to Stop Snoring

An off-beat cure for snoring has been developed by an Irish doctor.

The physician reported considerable success in overcoming the noisy practice by having his patients bite on a piece of wood for 5 minutes before going to sleep. His 18-month study involved some 500 persons.

He said that gnawing on a hard substance tires the jaw muscles and that this tends to reduce snoring.

A cure for snoring may not put much of a dent in solving the big problems that face the world today. Nevertheless whatever is done to make daily living more peaceful certainly has some merit.

Man goes to great lengths to safeguard and promote his material comforts and security. In the proper perspective, this is important and justifiable.

But greater attention should be given to the spiritual well-being of all. It is here that the great unfinished business of our time is found—and here that the Lord wants you to make some positive contribution.

✧

*"The good man out of the good treasure of his
heart produces good."*   [LUKE 6:45]

✧

Help me come to grips with the challenges of
our nuclear age, O Lord, and do something
about them.

Gap Widens between "Haves" and "Have-Nots"

Every day 30,000 children die of hunger and preventable disease.

Every year 16,000,000 babies die before reaching their first birthday.

In some low-income countries, the death rate of children is 40 times higher than it is in the U.S.

These facts, listed by an international children's organization, are followed by this warning: "In recent years the gap has actually been widening, not narrowing, between the standard of living in the low-income and high-income areas of the world. This creates dangerous tensions among peoples."

Because most of us are blessed with abundance, God expects us to assume responsibility for achieving a better balance in the world.

The poet John Donne proclaimed our personal involvement in meeting the world's needs when he wrote:

"Any man's death diminishes me, because I am involved in mankind. And therefore, never ask for whom the bell tolls —it tolls for thee."

✧

"None of us lives to himself, and none of us dies to himself."   [ROMANS 14:7]

✧

Open my eyes and my heart, Jesus, to my duty to the poor, the under-educated and the forgotten.

87

New Horizons for Men 65 and Over

Hiring men over 65 as toll collectors has worked so well for the Garden State Parkway in New Jersey that the program is being expanded.

Several years ago, State highway authorities sought to help older men supplement their social security benefits and at the same time find responsible employees.

A start was made by employing a dozen men over the usual retirement age. The project was so successful that the State set about to find 50 more. They normally work from 4 to 6 hours a day during peak traffic periods and earn up to $2300 a year.

A humane consideration for the needs of elder citizens is an enlightened and important work.

Anything you can do to show respect, encouragement and provide useful employment for others, young or old, will be richly rewarded by Him Who is the Father of us all.

Whatever you are able to accomplish may have far-reaching effects for good.

✧

"They shall bring forth fruit in old age."
[PSALM 92:14]

✧

Spur me, O Holy Spirit, to help older persons
make their rightful contributions to the good
of all.

The Art of Asking Questions

What is the difference between an outstanding teacher and a mediocre one? It's the ability to ask intelligent, well-prepared questions, according to Prof. Abraham Bernstein of Brooklyn College.

"When the wise teacher speaks, it should be chiefly to raise questions," he said. "What differentiates a wise question from a foolish one is the degree of forethought and preparation presented in the question."

Prof. Bernstein went on to say that the best sort of question is troublesome and not easy to answer.

"The poor teacher seeks for answers, any answers, to fill the vacuum, but the wise teacher strolls, and does not rush, toward answers."

It requires a deep faith in the God-given abilities of young people to ask questions that might stump them. But the rewards can be as inspiring as they are surprising.

Whether you are a teacher, student, parent or interested onlooker, do what you can to build for the future by strengthening the educational process here and now.

✧

"Take thought for what is noble in the sight of all."   [ROMANS 12:17]

✧

Guide all teachers to instruct wisely, O Lord of wisdom, and inspire all students to learn well.

Temper Enthusiasm, Don't Stifle It

Tumbling 50 feet over a gorge at Niagara Falls, a 5-year-old boy grabbed onto a tree and waited 60 long minutes for help.

While hundreds of anxious spectators gathered below, a member of the police rescue squad inched his way up a 100-foot incline and brought the lad to safety.

Aside from minor cuts and bruises, including a chipped tooth, the boy was declared fit.

He later explained that he had been playing with his 3-year-old sister at a 4-foot retaining wall, when he climbed over the barrier and then lost his footing.

The enthusiasm of the young has to be guided as well as moderated. To repress it entirely would be as much a mistake as to allow it full and unrestricted play.

Far from resenting reasonable restraints, most young people welcome them, if accompanied by a solicitude rooted in love.

God will bless your every effort to set proper limits to youthful zeal instead of holding it back.

✧

"Listen to me . . . O children; and act accordingly, that you may be kept in safety."

[SIRACH 3:1]

✧

Endow me with a sense of balance, O Holy Spirit, in protecting my own best interests and those of others.

Man Sorry after Rampage

Regret came a bit late for one man who did the following things after a quarrel with his sister.

He became so angry that he:

- kicked in the television set;
- destroyed the radio;
- ripped the headboard off a bed;
- broke a glass door panel;
- damaged the refrigerator;
- wrecked the washing machine;
- wrenched 2 legs off a table;
- smashed the glass door of a china cabinet;
- broke down the front door.

"I'm sorry," was all he could say after being brought into court.

Apologies can be helpful in making the best of a bad situation—or they can be a weak attempt to find an easy way out. At most, they come a little late.

Rather than allow yourself to become involved in situations where regret becomes necessary, ask for God's help to do the right thing the first time.

✧

"Do not let the sun go down on your anger."
[EPHESIANS 4:26]

✧

Make me realize, O Lord, that I will be judged on my actions, not by my unfulfilled intentions.

Do You "Get Through" to Others?

The word "communicate" deserves more than passing reflection by anyone who wishes to play a constructive role on the stage of life.

It is derived from "cum" meaning "with" and "unio" signifying "oneness" or "union." "Communicate" in its general sense means to do something to get closer to others. This can be done by passing on factual, helpful information to them, thus possessing it in common with them.

The dictionary defines "communicate" in several ways such as these: "to transmit, impart, make known, as to communicate news, or an idea . . . to interchange thought or intelligence by speech or writing."

It is part of your mission in life to be a communicator, to share with other persons the truth, both human and divine, rather than keep it to yourself.

If you remember that the Lord sends some of His love and truth to others through you, then you are more likely to be an effective communicator.

✧

"Speak the truth to one another, render in your gates judgments that are true and make for peace." [ZECHARIAH 8:16]

✧

May I always strive to share with others, O Jesus, the truth You entrust to me.

History's Great Men Overcame Hardship

Beethoven composed most of his music only after he lost his hearing at the age of 32.

- Alexander Graham Bell was laughed at for his invention of the telephone as "a crank who says he can talk through a wire."
- Clara Barton, who organized the American Red Cross in the heat of Civil War battles, had to overcome a timid nature that made her, as a child, "a shrinking bundle of fears."
- Francis Parkman became America's first great historian despite a nervous disorder which he painfully surmounted by writing his volumes on a wooden frame guided by wires.
- Louis Braille, developer of the braille system of reading for the blind, was sightless himself.
- Dostoevski survived 4 years in a Siberian prison camp and the afflictions of epilepsy to become one of the world's greatest novelists.
- St. Paul generously endured endless sufferings to bring Christ to all men: *"We are afflicted in every way, but not crushed; perplexed, but not driven to despair; persecuted, but not forsaken."* [2 CORINTHIANS 4:8,9]

✧

Spur me, heavenly Father, to actively imitate
those who showed greatness in every age.

Suicide Can Be Prevented

Each year some 200,000 Americans try to take their own lives. Thirty thousand or more actually succeed in committing suicide.

In citing these figures, statistician Dr. Louis I. Dublin told the American Public Health Association that much can be done by communities, groups and individuals to rescue the would-be suicide "by offering a helping hand." If people who are emotionally or mentally upset can get help and sympathy, Dr. Dublin added: "Experience has shown that suicide is, to a degree, at least, a preventable condition."

There are very few human problems that cannot be solved by people motivated by a divine desire to be of service to others and willing to accept the difficulties involved.

If you regard it as both a privilege and responsibility to act as God's agent in helping those less fortunate, you will welcome opportunities to give of your time and talents rather than close your eyes to the needs of those in trouble.

❖

"Bear one another's burdens, and so fulfill the law of Christ."　　　　[GALATIANS 6:2]

❖

Help me to realize, O divine Master, that in serving those in need I am honoring You.

How to Give Advice

An alert bus driver shot this friendly question at a man who was grouchy with him and his fellow passengers:

"Did you quarrel with your wife this morning?"

"Yes," the man admitted with surprise.

"That's your private affair," the driver quietly remarked, "why make it public?"

"Sorry," the passenger said—and smiled.

It isn't always that a person receives helpful advice in such a palatable manner. On the other hand, most of us tend to make suggestions when they are not sought or in a way calculated to annoy rather than convince.

The ability to give a tactful hint to an erring associate—and to take advice, too—hinges largely on how sincerely we respect and love others.

Frankly acknowledge your own defects before God and try to correct them in dealing with your fellow men. Then you will secure a better hearing when you have some constructive suggestion to make.

✧

"For this slight momentary affliction is preparing for us an eternal weight of glory beyond all comparison." [2 CORINTHIANS 4:17]

✧

Help me not to minimize my own faults, O Holy Spirit, nor to exaggerate those of others.

95

Airborne by Her Powerful Tresses

Raised 75 feet aloft by the hair of her head, one 20-year-old circus performer astonishes audiences daily by her death-defying gyrations.

To the rhythmic beat of music far below, the strong-haired miss rolls hoops on her legs, juggles clubs and balls simultaneously and goes through the intricate movements of a ballerina.

"I've been around for more than 40 years," explains one of the circus employees, "saw them all on swinging and flying trapeze, but this girl matches the best of them and maybe better."

Her long hair is woven into braids and attached by a rope to a ring high above. She can support her 120 pounds because of the extraordinary tensile strength of her tresses. Asked the secret of her success, the young woman replied: "Rehearse, rehearse."

Natural ability and constant practice are well-nigh unbeatable assets. If you add to these a determination to fulfill your obligations to God and man, you are on the high road to true achievement.

❖

"Be a vessel for noble use, consecrated and useful . . . ready for any good work."

[2 THESSALONIANS 2:21]

❖

Spur me on, O Lord, to use my talents for the common good of all.

Honesty in a Telephone Booth

A 10-year-old girl found $6.30 in nickels, dimes and quarters scattered over the floor of a telephone booth in New Jersey when she stepped into it to call her mother. The money had spilled over from a coin return slot.

After picking up the assortment of coins, she dialed the operator and asked what she could do to get them back to the telephone company. The operator instructed her how to feed the money back into the coin box.

When the child was commended for returning the money, she said: "I never thought of keeping it."

The New Jersey Bell Telephone Co. invited the youngster for lunch and a tour of its headquarters as a token of the company's appreciation for her honesty.

A simple example such as this is heartening evidence of the fact that the inclination to "do good and avoid evil" is deeply ingrained in man's nature by his Creator. It can never be completely ignored or eliminated.

No matter how grim things may seem at times, there is solid reason for hope in the fact that this divine impulse always lingers in men.

✧

"Let love be genuine; hate what is evil, hold fast to what is good." [ROMANS 12:9]

✧

Let me honor You, O my Redeemer, by being honest under all circumstances.

97

In 50 Years—What Kind of World?

A half-century from now, average citizens may earn $20,000 a year, jet around the world with ease and have a life of unprecedented leisure and luxury.

So predicts a noted scientist—Dr. Herman Kahn of the Hudson Institute.

But not everything foreseen by Dr. Kahn is this rosy. The technological revolution can bring dangers as well as blessings.

High on the list of threats will be the possible invention of a "doomsday machine" capable of destroying all human life. Even the waste heat from huge cities and sky jet-lanes may upset the delicately balanced processes of weather.

Looking into the future is a risky and often disquieting business. But man's questing mind must keep pushing back new horizons.

The stakes for personal and global survival keep getting higher. God's greatest gift—His own love shared with man for the sake of other men—will never fail to supply the chance for the moral growth we need.

✧

"He destined us in love to be His sons through Jesus Christ, according to the purpose of His will." [EPHESIANS 1:5]

✧

Let us all mature, Lord, as citizens of a single race headed for the same divine destiny.

Handwriting Makes a Difference

Poor penmanship causes plenty of trouble.

- A delivery man in Washington, D.C., for instance, misread a scribbled order for fuel oil and pumped 385 gallons through a disconnected intake into the basement of a house from which the tank had been removed.
- A bank in Philadelphia has a large "Who am I?" account for money turned in with unreadable deposit slips.
- A customer who sent an order to a department store for slippers with zippers got sleepers with grippers.

The toll resulting from bad handwriting costs Americans about $70 million a year. Scrawled bills, orders, tickets, invoices and checks create waste, confusion and ill will.

Carelessness in small matters does more than hamper personal development. Chain-reaction effects trigger inconvenience and hardships for countless others.

Ask God to help you do little things well and you will be preparing yourself for the bigger challenges of life.

✧

"To act faithfully is a matter of your own choice." [SIRACH 15:15]

✧

Enlighten me, O Holy Spirit, so that I may see the far-reaching effects of even the smallest efforts.

Loving Care for Tiny Patients

The affectionate title of "play lady" is given by young patients to a special hospital worker at the San Francisco Medical Center.

Her job is to "try to help the frightened child and his worried parents adjust to illness and hospitalization," as one social group worker put it.

She has a special playroom for the little ones with toys, crafts, games, books and music. They provide a familiar link with home and offer ways of releasing anxiety.

Separation from parents is the most worrisome thing to younger children, it was pointed out by the "play lady." Fear of physical disfigurement and lack of privacy also bother the sensitive adolescent in a special way, she added.

The need for a sense of security is a basic, universal one, particularly in children.

Anyone who cooperates with parents in providing little ones with a happy environment that is relatively free from fear is doing the Lord's work.

❖

"Whoever receives one such child in My name receives Me." [MARK 9:37]

❖

Let me do my part, Father, to calm the fears of those who are disturbed.

Stretcher Case Suddenly Revives

Dedicated firemen, responding to an emergency ambulance call, carefully carried a sick man on a stretcher down two flights of twisting stairs.

On reaching street level, they paused to rest, cautiously lowering the stretcher to the floor. Its occupant spied some mail in his box and, as the firemen watched in astonishment, he got up, took the mail and then lay down again, remarking: "I might want to read this in the hospital."

Self-interest can stimulate people to do amazing things. Once the want is strong enough, seemingly overwhelming obstacles become comparatively insignificant.

However selfish the motivation, it remains positive evidence of an inner power waiting to be tapped.

While giving due attention to actual needs of body, mind or soul, make sure that your imagination does not exaggerate little weaknesses.

Instead of favoring your personal troubles and difficulties, show a Christlike concern for those of others, and you'll probably forget about your own.

✧

"You shall love your neighbor as yourself."
[LEVITICUS 19:18]

✧

Grant, O Jesus, that I may show the same solicitude for the wants of others as I do for my own.

Crow Saves Life of Pup

A crow became a puppy's best friend when the little dog was caught in an animal trap in Zambia, Africa.

Both animals were pets of a couple living temporarily in a road construction camp.

Shortly after the puppy disappeared, they noticed that their crow was not eating normally. It would take a bit of food from its dish and then fly off with it in its beak only to return soon again to fetch another scrap of food.

Puzzled, the couple decided to follow the crow as it started off again with a choice piece of meat. They soon discovered that the crow had led them to the spot where their pet puppy was trapped. They found the little dog in perfect health.

According to a zoo official, crows are known to form unusual friendships and when put to the test are faithful and courageous allies.

How much more should intelligent human beings, made in God's image, show a warm and persevering solicitude when their fellow men are in trouble.

✧

"You yourselves have been taught by God to love one another." [1 THESSALONIANS 4:9]

✧

Teach me to excel, O Savior, in helping others in need.

The Mail Didn't Get Through

A young mailman who lacked the usual dedication of the typical letter carrier took the easy way out one day when he couldn't complete his daily rounds before dark.

Instead of returning his undelivered mail to the post office, he hid it in trees, hedges, boxes and even the public library.

Following up on complaints about missing mail, a post office inspector found a batch of letters in the library hiding spot. He soon traced down the procrastinating postman who disclosed the various spots where he had deposited his mail.

When found guilty before the court, the letter carrier said: "I was afraid to take them back to the post office because I felt my bosses were dissatisfied when I returned with undelivered letters."

Be motivated by divine love of people rather than by selfish fear. Then you will show by your thoughts, words and deeds that you are animated by a sense of responsibility to others, not dominated by self-interest.

✧

"If any man would come after Me, let him deny himself, and take up his cross, and follow Me." [MARK 8:34]

✧

May I always keep in mind the rights of others, O Lord, while seeking my own legitimate interests.

APRIL 4

In Which Category Do You Belong?

There are 3 kinds of people in the world, according to the late Nicholas Murray Butler, former president of Columbia University.

- the doers—the few people who make things happen;
- the onlookers—the many who watch things happen;
- the uninterested—the overwhelming majority who have no idea of what is happening.

Life becomes more interesting—and so do you—if you strive with God's help to join the ranks of the "doers."

Stimulate others as well to do more than sit on the sidelines during these challenging times.

Keep reminding them in a tactful but persistent manner that every person is needed in the never-ending task of changing the world for the better.

You can help many to shift from passive indifference to constructive involvement. Every prayer, word and deed can count for the benefit of all.

✧

"Be the more zealous to confirm your call and election."　　　　　　　　[2 PETER 1:10]

✧

Inspire me, O Holy Spirit, to be a doer, not a mere spectator on the stage of life.

Commitment Means Giving of Self

Many people complain about the aimlessness and emptiness in their lives. They fail to realize that they lack commitment to anything outside themselves.

John Gardner referred to this need when he said: "Our society not only fails to ask for or expect any depth of commitment from the individual; in a curious way it even discourages such commitment."

The origin of the word "commitment" may help you to add direction and purpose to your own life as well as to assist others to do the same.

It comes from "*cum*" (with) and "*mittere*" (to send). "Commitment" means to freely "send" or "pledge" oneself with deep conviction to a person, idea or cause.

In the design of God every person has a vocation to make his own unique contribution to life.

Commit yourself generously to the never-ending task of bringing divine love into a world sorely in need of it. Then you will achieve self-fulfillment and experience the true joy of living.

❖

"By this we know love, that He laid down His life for us; and we ought to lay down our lives for the brethren."   [1 JOHN 3:16]

❖

Inspire me, Holy Spirit, to find myself by giving of myself to others.

Teacher Is Taught Lesson

After 38 years, a teacher got a dose of her own medicine from a former pupil.

When she was brought into court for speeding, the judge recognized her as his high school freshman teacher. Recalling that she had once ordered all of her pupils to write 50 times: "I must not talk in class," he decided to give her a little reminder of old times. He sentenced her to write 100 times: "I must not exceed the speed limit."

Various methods can impress a sense of responsibility on human beings. Yet effective as they may be, there is no substitute for self-discipline.

Until a person sincerely decides to correct his own shortcomings, there is little assurance of real repentance or the enduring determination needed to right what is wrong in one's self.

Perfecting yourself is the life-long task assigned to you by Almighty God. He will give you all the help you need to bring out the best that is in you during your pilgrimage to heaven.

✧

"You, therefore, must be perfect, as your heavenly Father is perfect." [MATTHEW 5:48]

✧

Teach me, O Holy Spirit, to master myself and thus be better fitted to bring out the best in others.

A Hand-Dug Oil Well

Digging an oil well by hand was one man's way of meeting an emergency.

The setting was Wyoming where tall oil rigs are a common sight. But all were in use and he had to act quickly. The lease on his property faced cancellation a few days later unless drilling began.

A survey indicated possible oil-bearing sands at depths of 20 to 30 feet. So he went to work with pick and shovel—and soon struck oil at 21 feet.

To remove the oil, he set up a one-cylinder motor taken from a washing machine. It powered a small pump jack that brought in 5 barrels a day.

When a person sets his mind on any goal well worth achieving, he is apt to tap remarkable powers of imagination and resourcefulness.

Keep ever before you the ultimate goal of your life—the very purpose of your existence. Then you are more likely to develop a spirit of enterprise that may put you on the high road to heaven.

✧

"Straining forward to what lies ahead, I press on toward the goal for the prize of the upward call of God in Christ Jesus."
[PHILIPPIANS 3:13]

✧

Keep me alert, O divine Master, to opportunities to do good for others as well as myself.

Jesus' Parting Words

Never in all their experience with the Master did the Apostles hang so intently on His words as they did at the Last Supper. The air was charged with a sense of impending tragedy. And yet buoying up each of them was an indefinable spirit of fraternal love which they would never forget.

Jesus' words, as set down in the Gospel of John, carried many lessons. Here are a few of them, which were intended not only for the disciples but also for all who, as He put it, "believe in Me through their word." [JOHN 17:20]

He told them to serve, not dominate—"If I then, your Lord and Teacher, have washed your feet, you also ought to wash one another's feet." [13:14]

He gave them the mark of the disciple—"By this all men will know that you are My disciples, if you have love for one another." [13:35]

He gave them a new title—"No longer do I call you servants . . . but I have called you friends." [15:15]

He assured them of victory—"But be of good cheer, I have overcome the world." [16:33]

He prayed to the Father for unity—". . . that they may become perfectly one." [17:23]

❖

Help me, O Holy Spirit, to work tirelessly for the unity of all men according to the divine Will.

Goodness Found Where Least Expected

Unlikely people spoke up in behalf of Jesus on Good Friday during His passion and death.

One was Pontius Pilate's wife who, being married to the Roman governor, was herself a pagan. "While he (Pilate) was sitting on the judgment seat, his wife sent word to him, 'Have nothing to do with that righteous man, for I have suffered much over Him today in a dream.' "

[MATTHEW 27:19]

Another was the Roman centurion, the commander of a company of infantry: "When the centurion saw what had taken place, he praised God, and said, 'Certainly this man was innocent.' "

[LUKE 23:47]

Then too there was the thief who hung with Jesus on the cross. He rose above his own agony to defend the innocence of the Savior. Then he heard this joyful promise of Christ: "Truly, I say to you, today you will be with Me in paradise."

[LUKE 23:43]

Such goodness in persons who might otherwise be considered far from God should spur us to imitate the Lord in loving every human being.

✧

Keep me, Lord, from self-righteousness in my dealing with each person I encounter in life.

The Message of Holy Saturday

Silent mourning, reflection and hope are the marks of Holy Saturday.

There is mourning because He who came as the Light of the World has been taken away in death. The thought of anyone's dying, let alone that of God's Son, calls for sorrow in the hearts of thinking men.

There is reflection because the Lord had foretold His violent end. "Behold, we are going up to Jerusalem," He had told His apostles, "and everything that is written of the Son of man by the prophets will be accomplished. For He will be delivered to the Gentiles, and will be mocked and shamefully treated and spit upon, they will scourge Him and kill Him, and on the third day He will rise again." [LUKE 18:31–33]

There is hope because He predicted that He would arise and, faith tells us, He did. But as St. Paul reminded the Romans [8:24], "Hope that is seen is not hope."

It remains for us to carry the faith, hope and love of Christ into a world in danger of perishing without Him.

✧

Never let me become discouraged, O Lord, by the tragedies of life, for Your death has won us the victory.

Reflections on Easter Sunday

Easter is the feast of our liberation.

The Easter Gospel "He is risen!" is the center and core of belief of all who follow Christ.

Easter is a celebration of an event that actually happened, not just a beautiful story.

But it is far more than a recalling of the past, such as the Fourth of July.

It is the conquest of sin, death and the fear of evil—known and unknown.

This is so despite the very real problems and even tragedies that afflict so many people.

Easter proclaims that, just as Jesus has risen by the Father's power, we too will rise to a new kind of life. In a way this has already begun.

Many have never heard the Easter message. Others, through indifference or sorrow, find it unbelievable. If those for whom the Resurrection is a living reality bring it into the marketplace where human need is the greatest, then the joy of Easter can be communicated to all men.

✧

"Christ has been raised from the dead, the first fruits of those who have fallen asleep."
[1 CORINTHIANS 15:20]

✧

Make me more aware of Your active presence, Lord, and share this experience with many others.

Airline Stewardess' Last Letter

Shortly before she was killed in an airplane crash several years ago, Patricia Stermer, an airline stewardess, sent what proved to be her last letter to her mother and father in Gladbrook, Iowa.

This excerpt from the 21-year-old girl's letter reveals an inspiring devotion to her parents.

"You never leave me when I'm flying, working, playing, sleeping," she wrote. "No girl has more to be thankful for than I! Mother, you have given me so many standards to build my life upon. Daddy, you are so truthful and good, you have set a wonderful example for me.

"My life will not be a selfish one," she continued. "With God's help I shall be a better person for this period in my life. Again, you are the center of my existence. If your job as parents could be measured by the love, devotion and deep respect I hold for you, then dear ones, you indeed have done yourselves proud . . ."

Whether you are parent or child, do what you can to strengthen family life and you will be doing the work of God.

✧

"Honor your father and mother."
[EXODUS 20:12]

✧

Bless all parents, O Jesus, who strive perseveringly to instill in their children a sense of loyalty and devotion.

Grateful Collegians Remember Landlady

A large room and bath—rent free—has been the yearly gift of a Baltimore woman to needy Johns Hopkins University students since 1947.

Years later, Mrs. William Whitridge still receives mail from her dozen grateful boarders. They include professors, businessmen, scientists and an editor—some from as far as Afghanistan, Ethiopia and Hungary.

Besides providing the room, Mrs. Whitridge kept her boarders well-fed, coached some in fine points of grammar and others in table manners. She even helped one struggling student to overcome a speech defect.

"I wish more people would open their homes to outstanding young men who need help," was her comment.

When you get right down to it, there are only two forces in the world—love and hate. In varying degrees, each leaves a mark on those it touches.

Your scope may be no greater than that of the kindly Baltimore woman. But, in God's goodness, who can tell how far your love-based actions may extend?

✧

"Do not neglect to show hospitality to strangers." [HEBREWS 13:2]

✧

Where there is indifference or hatred, Lord, let me sow love.

Singing to Hens Increases Egg Laying

Because their owner sings to her hens, they lay far more eggs. This is the claim of a poultry farm owner in Stoneleigh, England. The 30-year-old woman owns 6,000 hens that have an amazing record—90 eggs daily for each 100 hens.

"It's the singing that does it," said the young woman. "Hens respond to singing just as cows do to music. Many farmers in Britain play recorded music to boost milk production."

She maintains that hens are not alone in appreciating thoughtfulness. "I have learned that all living things respond if you treat them properly."

However imperfectly we may succeed, each of us should strive to imitate the Lord Whose love for all of creation knows no bounds.

Keep alert for opportunities to show a particular consideration for any of your fellow human beings in physical or spiritual need. This goes especially for those who are unable to make any return to you.

✧

"Fear not; you are of more value than many sparrows." [LUKE 12:7]

✧

Help me, O Master, to develop a greater love for Your creatures.

Income Taxes Bring on Insomnia

Sleepness nights and income taxes seem to go together for more than a few people.

One man, however, who tried to solve his tax problems and his insomnia, wrote the Bureau of Internal Revenue: "I am enclosing $28.00. I haven't been able to sleep for the last four years because I cheated the government out of $56.00 on my income tax."

And then he added: "If I find I still can't sleep, I'll send you the other $28.00."

Paying taxes is seldom a pleasant duty. But until another and better way of providing the essential services of good government is found, every citizen is expected to shoulder his fair share of the tax burden.

Those who dodge their tax obligations might think twice if they would stop to realize the consequences of their selfish omission. They leave it to others to pay for the privileges of the liberty they enjoy.

Show that you appreciate the freedom God wishes each of us to possess by cheerfully fulfilling the responsibilities that accompany every right.

✧

"Pay all of them their dues, taxes to whom taxes are due, revenue to whom revenue is due." [ROMANS 13:7]

✧

Grant, O Lord, that I may conscientiously live up to my obligations as a good citizen.

Love—And Be Loved

Dolly Madison, wife of the fourth President of the United States, was one of the most popular women in American history.

Wherever she went, she charmed and captivated one and all—obscure and well-known, rich and poor, men and women alike.

She was once asked to explain the secret of her power over others. Surprised at the question, Mrs. Madison exclaimed: "Power over people! I have none. I desire none. I merely love everyone."

Those who love all people without exception are usually richly rewarded by the love they receive in return.

Every one of us without exception is capable of being an instrument of God's love.

In fact, it is our chief mission in life to apply divine love to every area of human life as far as we can reach.

It is a God-like work that enriches the lives of others as well as our own.

❖

"If we love one another, God abides in us and His love is perfected in us." [1 JOHN 4:12]

❖

May I draw others to You, O Lord, by my love for them.

Sculptor Works on Old Junk

One man's junk is another man's sculpture, judging by the achievement of one artist in Dobbs Ferry, N.Y.

The sculptor, a former opera singer, fashions iron statues out of the parts of old washing machines, cars, tractors, plows, hay rakes and broken tools.

His favorite hunting ground is an area in Maine where abandoned farms and old, broken farm machinery are plentiful.

With hammer and welding tools, the sculptor makes artifacts from discarded materials, such as a ballet dancer from a sewing machine, a rooster from a hay rake and the wings of a bird from a plowshare.

The transformation of seemingly useless objects into things of beauty takes place in the creative genius of man before it becomes reality.

Thank God for the unique contribution to life that each person can make. Try to foster a love for art, which is a reflection of His glory, in everyone you can reach.

✧

"From the greatness and beauty of created things comes a corresponding perception of their Creator."   [WISDOM 13:5]

✧

Open my eyes, O Holy Spirit, to the wonders of nature and man's potential for creativity.

Cheers up Subway Riders

The cheerful courtesy of a subway token seller unobtrusively brightens the lives of thousands of New York City commuters.

When interviewed at his change booth, the worker said that his customers respond warmly to his greetings of "Good morning!" "Have a pleasant trip!" and a variety of thoughtful compliments.

"Some are taken aback at first," he said, "but after their initial surprise they take it for granted and are friendly back."

"People have their problems," he continued, "but an early morning smile can't hurt them. In fact, I think it helps. I like my job, and part of that job is to try and make the passengers happy."

Don't underestimate the value of using countless little opportunities in daily activities to be an instrument of God's love.

If you strive in small ways and large to bring happiness and joy into the lives of others, you will add a new dimension to your own life.

✧

"A *pleasant voice multiplies friends, and a gracious tongue multiplies courtesies.*"

[SIRACH 6:5]

✧

Teach me, O divine Master, to cheer up people rather than depress them.

You Must Make the First Move

These lines entitled, "It's up to You," were penned by a man who is trying to do his part to stir up a sense of personal responsibility.

> You are the fellow who has to decide,
> Whether you'll do it or toss it aside,
> You are the fellow that makes up your mind,
> Whether you'll lead or linger behind,
> Whether you'll try for a goal that's afar,
> Or just be contented to stay where you are.
> Take it or leave it, there's something to do,
> Just think it over—it's all up to you.

It's a human tendency to shirk responsibility, but disaster invariably results when the good people take care of themselves and leave the running of the world to those who are not so good.

Face up to the hazards of freedom cheerfully, courageously and conscientiously. But remember nobody can force you to do this. Even the Lord Himself leaves it up to you!

❖

"Each tree is known by its own fruit."

[LUKE 6:44]

❖

Thanks, O Jesus, for the privilege of playing any role, however small, in renewing the face of the earth.

Man Should Know Better

A fish within a fish provided an unexpected dividend for a lucky angler in Hawaii.

After he hooked a 670-pound marlin, it became entangled in the rocks. A companion went overboard and looped a rope around the fish's tail.

When the marlin was landed, a 30-pound dolphin popped from its throat.

In a world where big fish eat little fish and the strong frequently overpower the weak, the importance of upholding moral values becomes greater, not less.

While the balance of nature demands that certain animals and fish become food for others, with man it is otherwise.

Thanks to reason, illumined by God's word, man can make his way through life, not only avoiding harm to others, but even "losing" himself that they may gain.

In fact, there is no better manner in which a person can get beyond half-living than by a Christlike regard for other human beings, whether they are poor, exploited, excluded or denied the benefits of religion.

✧

"Let us set an example to our brethren, for their lives depend upon us."   [JUDITH 8:24]

✧

Make me live, O Jesus, not by the law of the jungle but by the law of Your love.

120

Leaves Large Sum to His City

An elderly man left his entire estate of $200,000 to the city of Norwalk, Conn.

In his will, the 82-year-old benefactor wrote: "Norwalk has been good to me; I want the city to have everything." In this case "everything" consisted of $40,000 in real estate and $160,000 in personal property, cash and investments.

For many years the appreciative old man lodged in furnished rooms. It was only the year before his death that he bought a house for himself.

While you may be neither disposed nor able to provide more than your own small share of support for government, remember that it is your government just as much as it is anyone's.

Show a patient, conscientious and constructive interest in sound politics, in voting in every election and in giving your moral support to upright, efficient candidates and officeholders. These are some of many ways that everyone can contribute to good government.

✧

"Let us then pursue what makes for peace and for mutual upbuilding."   [ROMANS 14:19]

✧

Thanks for the great blessing of liberty, O Lord. May I always be worthy of it.

The Days Are Getting Longer

Anyone wanting to squeeze more than 24 hours out of a day simply has to wait a few billion years.

According to a University of California professor the earth is rotating ever more slowly on its axis. This is caused by the friction due to the rising and falling of tides in the earth's crust and oceans.

In a half-billion years, the professor estimates, there will be 30 hours in a day—the time it takes for our planet to rotate once on its axis.

In 4½ billion years, he said, there will be as many as 200 hours in a day.

Time has a way of slipping past us, leaving behind a regretful memory of what might have been.

All the more valuable, then, is the advice of C. C. Colton (1780–1832) who said: "Much may be done in those little shreds and patches of time which every day produces, and which most men throw away."

Like every gift of God, time is to be used well. Crowd into the "shreds and patches" of each day some serious reading, thinking, prayer and kindness.

✧

"Walk, not as unwise men but as wise, making the most of the time." [EPHESIANS 5:15]

✧

Make me more aware of my final goal, Lord, so that I may use the days and years as stepping-stones to You.

Shaken by Skeleton

One look at a skeleton was enough to cause a woman to faint on a street corner in Port Elizabeth, South Africa.

An automobile happened to stop at the traffic light where she was waiting to cross a busy street. When she glanced at the car she saw the skeleton sitting on the back seat peering out at her. Then she keeled over.

The driver stopped to help the stunned woman and then explained: "This always happens whenever I take a skeleton to the workshop." He said that he was a technician at a medical supply concern and was transporting it from a hospital to his shop for repairs.

The unexpected appearance of a skeleton might send shivers down anyone's spine. But all of us need some reminder that sooner or later we will be summoned to appear before the Divine Judgment Seat and give an account of our stewardship.

Make the most of your fleeting years on earth. They count for eternity.

✦

"It is appointed for men to die once, and after that comes the judgment." [HEBREWS 9:27]

✦

Let me so live, O Lord, that I may always be prepared to die.

Squirrel Holds Record for Survival

Going 100 days without water is the rock squirrel's solitary claim to fame, according to a recent study.

The camel, which can live for about 30 days without a drink, is no match for this furry inhabitant of the American Southwest.

The rock squirrel is believed to be the world's champion among non-hibernating animals.

By nature animals are usually provided with the equipment they need for survival—whether it is swiftness, strength, ability to blend in with their surroundings or to live in a dry region.

Man, however, has a higher and more difficult calling. If he is to live happily, work effectively and be at peace with his fellow men, he must be willing to use his God-given talents in a way that requires the best resources of his mind and will.

Make every effort to guarantee, for others as well as yourself, not mere survival, but the reasonable sufficiency God intended for each person in your community, nation and world.

✧

"Agree with one another, live in peace and the God of love and peace will be with you."
[2 CORINTHIANS 13:11]

✧

Grant me the help I need, O Lord, to be at peace with all men, in so far as this is possible.

Space Research Can Be Boon for Mankind

The space program may save mankind tens of millions of dollars a year by helping use the earth's resources more efficiently.

This prediction was made by a rocket scientist, Dr. Werner Von Braun. He foresees the time when orbital surveys will spot mineral deposits, water supplies and belts of maximum fertility for crops.

"Whether the earth could support four times as many people is not the problem," the scientist commented in a magazine article. "It can. The problem is maintaining a balance between supply and demand."

Like any other scientific progress, the space program is capable of great benefit for all mankind, and not just the favored few in developed countries.

Will it be employed to feed the hungry, widen job opportunities, reduce ignorance and poverty? That is a human, rather than a scientific, question. God expects those in positions of responsibility to use technology for such ends, rather than exclusively for limited goals.

✧

"Rescue the weak and the needy."

[PSALM 82:3]

✧

Let me see in every human advance, Holy Spirit, an opportunity to further peace and justice.

Police Honor Courageous Teacher

A high school teacher faced dangerous odds when he came to the assistance of a traffic officer threatened by an angry mob while making an arrest in Seattle, Wash.

In presenting the history teacher with a certificate of merit, the chief of police said: "There have been many instances throughout the country where citizens have stood by and watched police officers resisted and injured without offering to give assistance."

Then he added, "We are proud to know that there are those in Seattle who will not let that happen."

The teacher responded: "This comes as an honor and a surprise, but one can't teach history and respect for law and order without living up to what one teaches."

Taking a stand for justice is seldom easy. But it is the responsibility of each person to do so if law and order rather than mob rule is to prevail.

God will bless you if you dare to champion the rights of your fellow man, especially when he is the victim of injustice.

❖

"You love righteousness and hate wickedness.
Therefore God, your God, has anointed you."
[PSALM 45:8]

❖

Teach me, O Holy Spirit, how to be brave without being reckless.

126

Success Story in India

A village in India that was on a waterless plain 10 years ago now has 6,000 acres of green fields of wheat, barley, mustard, rice and grapes.

Years of determined effort to dig irrigation wells have transformed Jorunda in Northwest India into a symbol of hope for the world's desolate areas.

Villagers look to the day when enough wells will be drilled to irrigate the town's entire 40,000 acres of arable land. Then it could supply not only its own food needs but those of surrounding areas.

Far better than merely giving handouts to the hungry is the use of research and ingenuity in helping solve the world's desperate food problem. Through improved methods of farming, irrigation, pest control and better fertilizers, ways can—and must—be found to provide the world's hungry with the standard of living God wishes all men to enjoy.

Awaken those around you to the great needs of the world which they can help fill through fitting themselves for work in vital fields.

✧

"He turns a desert into pools of water . . . and there He lets the hungry dwell."
[PSALM 107:35]

✧

Let me do all in my power, O Lord, to find practical ways to help meet the world food problem.

One Way to Solve a Problem

Golf champion Jack Nicklaus has won many tournaments not only by his skill but also by carefully analyzing and correcting his mistakes.

During one tournament, for instance, he looked for the best way to remedy his faulty putting. So he watched films taken earlier in the day in which he and other players appeared.

Nicklaus immediately recognized his defect. "I had been leaning over too far," he said. Before resuming the tournament the next day, he went out to the putting green and kept practicing until he eliminated the weakness.

A first step in solving any problem you may have is to check on yourself. This is seldom easy, for it is a failing of human nature to place blame at the doorstep of others rather than at our own.

God will bless and strengthen you if you are humble and honest enough to keep perfecting yourself by pinpointing your shortcomings and then rectifying them.

✧

"He leads the humble in what is right, and teaches the humble His way." [PSALM 25:9]

✧

Grant, O Lord, that I may be more interested
in correcting my own faults than in pointing
out those of others.

Boy's Interest Helps Classmates

The curiosity of a third-grader about his father's occupation set in motion a project that has shed a new light on education in one New York elementary school.

It began when the boy's father, a textile manufacturer, was explaining his business to his son. The boy asked his father to tell his classmates about his work.

After delivering his talk and asking for questions, the man related: "The response was astonishing. The hands kept flying up and I just had to keep talking."

The teacher was so enthusiastic that he requested the man to arrange for other parents to do the same.

Before long there was a regular assembly in which athletes, artists, businessmen, writers, actors and foreign envoys spoke of their own niche in life.

One way to inspire youngsters to take up a career in a needed field is to give them information and inspiration. The Lord will abundantly reward any effort you make to get even one young person started on a meaningful career.

✧

"If you are willing, my son, you will be taught." [SIRACH 6:32]

✧

Let me be an example to youth, O Lord, by showing them my own enthusiasm for a worthwhile life's work.

A Personal "Gold Flow" Problem

The elusive properties of money were made painfully clear to one woman who almost inadvertently whittled away the treasury of her bowling league.

When called to account for the $2,500 collected from the 60-member league, she could produce only $625.

The only explanation the embarrassed treasurer could give for the missing $1,900 was that it had "just trickled away" on household expenses.

Because she promptly made restitution of the money and pleaded guilty to petty larceny, the woman received a suspended sentence.

Theories about money and the various schools of economic thought are more abundant today than ever. Their relative merits may be profitably debated but one thing is certain: money doesn't last long unless it is handled with care and integrity.

You owe it to God, yourself, and those who depend upon you to earn your livelihood honorably, to save your money lawfully and to spend it wisely.

✧

"Let the thief no longer steal, but rather let him labor, doing honest work with his hands."
[EPHESIANS 4:28]

✧

Help me to regard money, O Lord, not as a master, but as a servant, in accomplishing worthwhile ends.

Quick Job by Helicopter

A helicopter lowered a 2,750-pound steel condenser through the roof of a factory in Yonkers, N.Y. The operation was so swift that it was completed before company officials could get to the roof to watch.

The 1,525 horsepower single-rotor helicopter rose above the buildings and gently lowered the apparatus through a pre-cut hole in the roof.

It took 10 minutes for the helicopter to do the job for a charge of $1,500.

Engineers said it would have taken a conventional crane three days at a cost of $5,000 to install the machine, which stands 13 feet high and four feet in diameter.

The increasing speed and efficiency that distinguishes our age puts us under greater obligation than ever. It is up to us to use our material blessings in a way that ennobles and liberates man rather than masters or enslaves him.

Thank God for the innumerable advantages of modern technology. Pray that all people, not merely the few, may share in these benefits.

✧

"He has filled them with ability to do every sort of work."   [EXODUS 35:35]

✧

Lord, may we always be worthy of the developing wonders of Your creation.

Settles a Long-Standing Debt

A long-standing debt was settled on a street corner, much to the surprise of the man who benefited by the transaction.

It happened when one man approached another in London, Kentucky, and asked him what his name was.

When he was told, the first man replied: "In 1928 I purchased a wagon bed iron from your father and never paid him. Now he's dead and I'm able to pay the $3.20."

Then he gave him the money and walked away.

Later the surprised recipient checked his father's old business records and—there was the debt.

Such occurrences are rare. But they are worthy of note when they do happen because they testify to the power of conscience that is in us all. Often it is the care with which we examine and weigh our daily actions prayerfully in the sight of God that makes the difference between a careful, correct conscience and a lax and faulty one.

Strive to obtain the knowledge needed to form your conscience objectively.

✧

*"I always take pains to have a clear conscience
toward God and toward men."* [ACTS 24:16]

✧

Help me acquire a conscience, O Holy Spirit,
that is truly Your word speaking to me.

Regains Sight after 60 Years

A 60-year-old Miami woman, who had been almost totally blind since she was 9 weeks old, suddenly regained her sight.

Since babyhood she had had only one per cent vision in her right eye. All she could distinguish was night from day.

One morning recently her left eye seemed moist and she casually rubbed it. Suddenly she saw the green linoleum in her kitchen.

Then she looked out the window and saw blue skies, trees and a chimney.

"A little glimpse of heaven," she described it.

And then speaking of the great blessing of sight that had been restored to her, she said: "I don't know how long it will last. Maybe a few days. Maybe a year. Maybe forever."

Pause occasionally to take stock of the numerous advantages of body and soul that God entrusts to you. Rather than take them for granted, show your gratitude by using them for the Lord and the good of others.

❖

"I was eyes to the blind, and feet to the lame."   [JOB 29:15]

❖

Thanks to You, O loving Father, for the blessing of sight.

$10,000 *Reward for Being Kind*

A little courtesy on the part of a supermarket department manager in Manhattan yielded a big return. An appreciative woman left him $10,000 in her will.

The surprised but grateful man recalled that his benefactress came to his produce department 2 or 3 times a week to buy fruits and vegetables. As with all his customers, the small bald man, with warm blue eyes and horn-rimmed glasses, made it a point to be pleasant and cooperative in helping her with purchases.

The 62-year-old man has been selling fruits and vegetables at the same stand for the past 16 years. Previous to that he worked at one spot for 25 years.

While we are all tempted at times to be grumpy, discourteous and rude, still it is within the power of every one of us, by the grace of God, to be kindly, well-disposed and sympathetic.

You may never get a remembrance in anybody's will for being cordial. But if you strive to bring the warmth of divine love into a world that quickly becomes cold and brutal without it, you will be rewarded for all eternity.

✧

"God is love, and he who abides in love abides in God, and God in Him."　[1 JOHN 4:16]

✧

Let me be an instrument of Your love, O Lord, in every situation possible.

Thousands of Ducks Perish

More than 8,000 ducks met a strange death on the Mississippi River recently.

In migrating north for the summer, they happened to alight on a stretch of the river that was coated with fuel oil and soy bean oil.

This freakish situation had been caused when a broken fuel pipe spilled a million gallons of oil into the water and a storage tank burst adding another million-and-a-half gallons of soy bean oil.

The ducks' feathers were so oil-soaked that they could neither fly nor float. Some were so weighted down that only their bills showed above the surface of the river.

Rescuers pulled piles of the dying ducks out of the water but only 500 lived.

Human error or negligence on the part of any one of us can have far-reaching repercussions.

Reflect frequently on this fact and you will have an added incentive for conscientiously fulfilling your responsibilities to God and all His creatures.

✧

"The earth He has given to the sons of men."
[PSALM 115:16]

✧

Inspire me, O Holy Spirit, to be aware of the consequences of all my thoughts, words and deeds.

Never Underestimate the Power of a Child

A child in his first 4 years has a greater potential for mental growth than most of us realize.

During this time he can increase his IQ at the rate of 2½ points each year. By the time he is 8, this has decreased to about half a point.

These findings of Dr. Benjamin Bloom of the University of Chicago underline the fact that the mind of a young child can learn much more than it is given credit for.

A proper home environment—one in which the child is encouraged to really look at and learn about the world around him—is the best possible atmosphere.

The child also has great spiritual potential at this early age. It is important, therefore, that his parents be concerned in a responsible way with the complete child, with his mind, his heart and his soul.

Help even the youngest children to expand their vision—to perceive the world of the spirit as well as the material attractions around them—so that they will grow in wisdom and grace.

✧

"Train up a child in the way he should go, and when he is old he will not depart from it." [PROVERBS 22:6]

✧

Let me be Your instrument, O Divine Savior, in opening the minds and hearts of children to You.

On Praise and Its Opposite

A female admirer ran up to a legislator after a speech and told him in an excited voice:

"Why, Congressman, your speech was superfluous, just superfluous!"

"Why, thank you," the lawmaker replied with a twinkle in his eye. "I'm thinking of having it published posthumously."

"Oh, wonderful!" was her instant reply.

As easy and tempting as it may be to believe readily every favorable report about our own performance, it is good sense to temper such a reaction with a generous dose of realism.

Most people are rarely as perfect as they think in their most elated moments or as bad as they imagine when they are depressed and despondent.

Since it is worth alone that matters in the sight of Almighty God, spend your time serving Him and your fellow man and you will not be unduly affected either by compliments or criticisms.

❖

"With me it is a very small thing that I should be judged by you . . . I do not even judge myself . . . It is the Lord who judges me." [CORINTHIANS 4:3,4]

❖

Inspire me always, O Christ, to refer my strong points to You and take the blame for my shortcomings.

Dish Damage Expensive

How many dishes and glasses are chipped or broken during a year in the United States? The total is some 960 million pieces, valued at $720 million, according to houseware researchers. "The typical family," the report stated, "washes around 20,000 dishes in a year's time and breaks or chips at least 24 dishes or glasses, costing about $16."

The statistics are based on reports of china and glassware merchandisers who deal continually with homemakers' purchasing replacements or new stock. Chipped or damaged items range in value from a 5¢ juice glass to a $25 serving platter. Cup handles are the biggest casualty. The kitchen sink where sudsy water makes dishes slippery is the place where most damage occurs.

As little chips, cracks and breaks of dishware can add up to a substantial loss, so can seemingly little moral infractions —multiplied by many people—hurt not only one person, but everybody else too.

Pay attention to the little things, then, realizing that in the divine plan they count for better or for worse.

✧

"In great or small matters do not act amiss."
[SIRACH 5:15]

✧

Teach me, O Jesus, to see the value of doing little things well.

Tiny Mother Gives Successful Birth

One of the world's smallest mothers is a tiny Australian woman only three feet tall.

Mrs. Grace Cook, 28, of Sydney gave birth to her second normal baby—a girl weighing 4 pounds 9 ounces. To prepare for the baby's birth, she had taken 10 weeks' physiotherapy before the delivery.

The program proved to be so successful that the diminutive woman felt better afterwards than many mothers almost twice her size.

Mothers come in all sizes and shapes. They are short and tall, attractive and plain, talkative and shy.

They speak English, French, Chinese, Russian and a thousand other languages and dialects.

They are brown, white, black and yellow.

They are Christian, Jewish, Moslem, Hindu, Buddhist—and other religions as well.

But what they have in common is a deep and abiding love for the children God has made theirs in a mysterious sharing of His own creative power.

✧

"All things come from You, and of Your own have we given You."   [CHRONICLES 29:14]

✧

Help mothers appreciate their privilege, Lord, and strengthen them to live up to its promise.

Make Every Conversation Count

Every conversation you have reveals something of your inner self. As Publilius Syrus said in 50 B.C., "Conversation is the image of the mind. As the man is, so is his talk."

Check occasionally on the conversations you have each day at home, on the job, in school, over the telephone, at meetings, social gatherings, on the bus or in the supermarket.

Ask yourself questions such as these:

- Do you see in each of your conversations an opportunity to share your good ideas with others? Or do they amount to little more than idle chatter?
- Do they reflect the best that is in you? Or the worst?
- Are you a good listener? Or do you tend to do most of the talking?
- Do you make it a point to be pleasant, considerate and helpful? Or don't you care?

Keep in mind that you can be the Lord's instrument in transmitting good ideas through conversation.

✧

"Pleasant words are like a honeycomb, sweetness to the soul and health to the body."
[PROVERBS 16:24]

✧

Let me speak to others, O Lord, as I wish they would speak to me.

Dropout Trains Youths

A former drifter is now training 60 "under-achievers" in the field in which he made good—marine biology.

The man now heads his own business in Florida. He is considered one of the foremost collectors of sea animals and fish, which he supplies to research laboratories all over the U.S.

Only a few years before, as a college dropout, he had been in much the same position as the young people he is presently helping. But, by reading everything he could find on sea animals and by steady practice he became expert in the subject.

"I am not setting myself up as an example to these kids," he said. "But I hope that they will see that they can learn even if they should decide to drop out of school and that they can make a career for themselves."

One of the most lasting contributions of one who has made a comeback is to be of practical help to those who want to do something with their lives. The Lord has put us on earth here to serve each other.

✧

"If anyone would be first, he must be last of all and servant of all."   [MARK 9:35]

✧

Strengthen us, Father, with hope for what we can accomplish with Your assistance.

Don't Underestimate Yourself

The bumblebee doesn't know it—but, according to the applied laws of aerodynamics, it should not be able to fly!

The size, weight and shape of this husky bee's body—in relation to its total wing-spread—indicate that it should never get off the ground.

Extensive laboratory tests and wind tunnel experiments by experts confirm this conclusion.

However, the bumblebee, unaware of these findings, continues to zoom through the air whenever and wherever it pleases.

No matter how others may rate your capabilities, do not underestimate any of the leadership skills you have.

The Lord has placed them in your keeping and He expects you to use them for the good of others as well as for yourself.

You may be pleasantly surprised that you can accomplish far more than you—or anyone else—imagines!

✧

"The bee is small among flying creatures, but her product is the best of sweet things."

[SIRACH 11:3]

✧

Thanks, O Father, for Your countless blessings.

Two Barriers to Success

Business executives received some advice from a doctor which can be profitably absorbed by us all.

In a talk to them, Dr. Francis J. Braceland suggested that those who had the "loneliness of command" must overcome 2 foes, namely "inordinate self-love and hostility."

"Both make it impossible," he added "to communicate properly with people in the environment and render one unable to see or feel relationships with others."

The doctor admitted this was difficult because "the duty and the power to direct the lives and fortunes of others is an awesome responsibility."

In the lives of each of us, the effective performance of our obligations may be threatened by the very same foes of self-love and hostility.

Take a few moments before almighty God to consider the plight we all would be in if everyone let such feelings overcome their better inclinations. Then resolve prayerfully to do in a spirit of joy what is rightly expected of you.

✧

"Let all bitterness and wrath and anger and clamor and slander be put away from you."
[EPHESIANS 4:31]

✧

Help me, O Lord, to keep myself open to Your help and not close myself to my fellow men.

Lions Cause Plane Scare

A frightened pilot radioed the control tower at the Brussels airport, "I have 3 lions in my cockpit!" He requested permission for an emergency landing. The control tower operator thought it was a joke, and replied: "Put them in your gas tank."

The operator was convinced, however, when he heard the unmistakable roar of a lion. The pilot had pushed the microphone toward one of the animals, which were being flown in a chartered cargo plane from Frankfurt to a London zoo.

As the co-pilot held the lions at bay with a fire-ax, the pilot landed. A woman zoologist, armed only with a broomstick and net, boarded the plane and coaxed the lions into crates.

Do not be surprised if people misunderstand you or do not take you seriously when you are in trouble. It is often hard for others to comprehend difficulties that are very immediate to you.

Ask God to keep you alert and sympathetic to the problems faced by your fellow man.

✧

"Do not grumble, brethren, against one another, that you may not be judged."

[JAMES 5:9]

✧

Deepen in me, O Holy Spirit, a practical concern for persons in danger.

Freedom Means Work

A social worker in Venezuela who is trying to stir up a sense of public responsibility, commented in a letter to us:

"It is encouraging that more and more people are getting together to do creative work in social fields. It's a good sign and I hope it continues."

Then she added: "Many people are becoming better aware of their duties in the political fields and women are really taking an active part."

Freedom, although God-given, depends on each of us. It is a fragile gift which we must preserve and fortify. Freedom is not for the lazy. It demands character, will and education. It requires decisions, self-respect and self-reliance.

A man must guard and preserve freedom just as he loves his home and children with a devotion that doesn't count either effort or sacrifice.

But the decision rests with you—and others like you—if future generations are to share in the blessed freedom that we enjoy in abundance.

❖

"So if the Son makes you free, you will be free indeed."   [JOHN 8:36]

❖

Let me show my appreciation of freedom, Lord, by seeking to extend its advantages to everybody.

Are You Prejudiced?

Are you inclined to jump to a conclusion before having the facts? If so, you are in danger of becoming prejudiced.

There's much food for thought in the origin of the word "prejudice." It comes from the Latin *"prae"* meaning "before" and *"judicium"* signifying "judgment."

In other words, to be prejudiced means to make up one's mind before taking into account all aspects of a situation.

The dictionary defines "prejudice" as "an unfavorable opinion or feeling formed beforehand—or without knowledge, thought or reason; any preconceived opinion or feeling."

If you wish to lead a worthwhile life, make it a strict habit to think, speak and act on knowledge or information that is based on the full truth, not on mere hearsay, sentiment or half-truths.

Be honest and fair with God, yourself, and your fellow man and there is little danger of your becoming prejudiced.

✧

"With the judgment you pronounce you will be judged." [MATTHEW 7:2]

✧

Help me, O Master, always to withhold judgment until I get all the facts.

Where There's a Will

A woman who supports herself by running a subway newsstand in New York also manages to finance an annual summer outing for 140 children and their mothers.

The thoughtful 54-year-old woman spends a good part of each year raising the $138 required to pay for two busses to transport the group to a suburban beach.

In addition to her regular supply of newspapers and periodicals, she also sells "back issues" which her customers donate toward raising the special fund.

They, too, wish to have a part in providing many children with their only chance to escape the summer heat of the city for at least one day.

Most of the world's problems could eventually be solved if enough persons in high positions and low used the imagination and talent God gave them to work on behalf of the less fortunate.

Any step you make in this direction is better than no step at all and could very well be a valuable contribution to the peace of the world.

✧

"Let not your hand be extended to receive,
but withdrawn when it is time to repay."
[SIRACH 4:31]

✧

Inspire me, O Holy Ghost, to show imagination helping those in need.

Students Have a Taste of Starvation

To find out how it feels to suffer from hunger, a college professor and 20 student volunteers—14 men and 6 women —underwent a 3-day fast at William Jewell College in Liberty, Mo.

The reason for the test was given by the professor, who said: "Half of the people of the world are hungry. We never have been and we don't know what it would feel like, so we decided to find out."

Limited to water and plain coffee or tea during the test, the participants found the experience a realistic one. A 19-year-old student, for instance, lost 9 pounds in 72 hours.

A senior said the fast was "highly worthwhile because it alerted all the students to the need of considering the world problem of hunger."

Helping the hungry people of the earth to help themselves is neither simple nor easy. But those who are blessed by the Lord with an abundance of food and the advantages of technology should make an endless effort to find permanent solutions.

✧

"For the needy shall not always be forgotten, and the hope of the poor shall not perish for ever."   [PSALM 9:18]

✧

Bless all, O Father, who strive to solve the problems of world hunger.

Diamond in the Garbage

This time it wasn't a needle in a haystack, but a diamond in a bargeload of trash and garbage that was the object of a frantic search.

The trouble started when a New York woman threw away a shopping bag. Shortly after the garbage collector had made his daily rounds, she suddenly recalled that she had left her $6,000 diamond ring, neatly wrapped in tissue paper in the bottom of the bag.

A phone call to the Sanitation Department produced quick results. Officials traced the garbage from the woman's home to an East River pier where an 800-ton barge was piled high with refuse.

Sanitation employees set to work to find the missing shopping bag. After rummaging through a huge assortment of garbage and trash, they finally discovered the bag—and the ring safe inside.

Make sure that you do not forget or overlook anything of value, especially if it concerns matters of the spirit. It may be much more difficult to recover than a diamond lost in the rubbish.

✧

"The kingdom of heaven is like a merchant in search of fine pearls." [MATTHEW 13:45]

✧

Watch over me, O gentle Master, and protect me from my own shortcomings.

Musician Trapped by Piano Stool

One embarrassed pianist was unable to stand for his final bow after playing a Mozart concerto in a Melbourne, Australia, concert hall.

His coattails had become caught in the piano stool. As a packed audience watched in bewilderment he wrenched, pulled and tugged—all to no avail.

Finally with a flourish, the quick-thinking pianist slipped out of his coat and took his bow in his starched white shirt front.

The audience roundly applauded both performances!

One basic ingredient of people who get things done is the willingness to forget self and concentrate on the work at hand. If the pianist had been overly concerned with his "dignity" he might have sat on the stool all night.

Seek the ever present aid of the Holy Spirit to grasp quickly which tasks most need to be performed at home, on the job, in the community or anywhere else. Then make serious efforts to forget self and set right what may need correcting.

✧

"Never flag in zeal, be aglow with the Spirit, serve the Lord." [ROMANS 12:11]

✧

Grant us the wisdom, Holy Spirit, to know the goals worth striving for, and then to attain them.

Exterminator Carried His Own Insects

Drumming up business was carried too far by one hardworking fellow who ended up in a Kentucky prison.

This is how it happened, as reported in the "Shop Column" of the jail's local magazine:

"Paul tells me he was a termite exterminator on the outside and had a successful business. He always carried a bottle of termites with him just in case he couldn't find any in the house to be treated."

Even those with a good head for business can carry their industriousness too far. Few would begrudge a hard worker the fruit of his labor, as long as it is done honestly, not deceitfully.

Those who are bent on self-aggrandizement seldom let up in their efforts. Such relentless pursuit of material things should prod the followers of the Lord to show equal vigor in pursuing higher objectives.

Whether you are a parent, teacher, public servant, office or factory worker or in any other occupation, persevere conscientiously in the good you have set out to accomplish.

✧

"Blessed are the pure in heart."

[MATTHEW 5:8]

✧

Give me a sturdy determination, O Holy Spirit, to keep going and never stop in the good work You have given me.

An Extra Can of Gasoline

An elderly man in Phoenix, Ariz., has found an off-beat but effective way to make the world a little better.

When a young man was taking his girl home one night from a dance, his car ran out of gas. The streets were empty and no service stations were open.

But the night was saved when an older man stopped, listened to their tale of woe and then did something about it. He took a two-gallon can of gasoline out of the back of his car and poured it into the stalled vehicle.

Refusing to accept money or to give his name, the benefactor simply said: "I carry gasoline all the time for stranded motorists. I wish others would do this and maybe we could spread some human brotherhood."

Carrying a gasoline can may not be your way of promoting the brotherhood of man under the fatherhood of God, but there is something you can do. Neglect no opportunity to take into your heart the problems of those who look to you for help.

✧

"Learn to do good."   [ISAIAH 1:17]

✧

For every blessing I receive from You, O Lord, let me return thanks by doing something for others.

Popularity Means Caring for Others

When asked "What qualities or characteristics make a teen-age girl popular?" high school students in St. Paul, Minn., gave the following answers:

"She usually thinks about others first."

"She's got to be considerate of others."

"She's interested in the people around her rather than herself."

Another said, "Popularity is just taking the time to get involved with people."

On the whole, the students considered popularity was more than "having a bubbling personality and a good sense of humor." They felt it also meant showing "consideration for another person's feelings, being genuinely interested in other people, easy to get along with and being involved."

Most of us, whether young or old, are usually conscious of the friendly attitude that others should display towards us. We should also keep in mind that the Lord expects us to show the same consideration for others.

✧

"Above all hold unfailing your love for one another." [1 PETER 4:8]

✧

Deepen in me, Jesus, an enduring solicitude for my fellow man.

They Brought Axes and Hammers

To help him wreck his studio, a London photographer invited 200 of his friends to bring axes and hammers to a special farewell party.

The unusual affair was the photographer's way of protesting against civic officials who gave him notice to quit his studio before the entire block was demolished to make way for a parking lot.

"We'll save them the trouble of knocking this place down," the man said. Then he assured each one of his invited guests that they would get a "big bang" out of his party.

Most people find momentary gratification in doing something destructive, whether it be in tearing down an old studio or in irresponsible fault-finding.

But the thrill is short-lived, because man by the very nature God gave him finds deep and lasting satisfaction only when he builds, not when he destroys.

Seek to devote your energies to the glory of God and the betterment of your fellow man and you will live a truly constructive and meaningful life.

✧

"Brethren, do not be weary in well-doing."
[2 THESSALONIANS 3:13]

✧

Grant, O Lord, that I may always build up rather than tear down.

Advice for Successful Salesmen

Salesmen who sell by phone were reminded of these courtesy tips in the Industrial Distributors News:

1. Allow time for the prospect or customer to answer the phone—there is nothing more annoying than to have the phone stop ringing just as you get to it.
2. Be ready to talk. Don't keep someone hanging on while you clear up last-minute duties.
3. Ask if it's convenient to talk. You would never think of breaking into a customer's office in person—don't do it by phone.
4. Listen. Inattentiveness shows over the phone just as it does in person.
5. Don't cause unnecessary delays. It's almost inexcusable to ask the customer to hold on, for example, while you get a piece of paper.

It is much easier to be courteous if we treat all people with the same thoughtfulness we expect from them.

Each of us can apply to situations of all kinds the divine standard of "doing unto others."

✧

"Practice these duties, devote yourself to them, so that all may see your progress."
[1 TIMOTHY 4:15]

✧

Let my sense of courtesy, Lord, spring from love of others for love of You.

Berry Pail Saves Man from Bear

Confronted by an angry bear, a 60-year-old man in Norway showed spur-of-the-moment resourcefulness that probably saved his life.

The big bear suddenly appeared when the man was out picking berries last summer. He realized that he had to act quickly to outsmart the animal.

Taking his berry bucket he managed to jam the handle of it over the bear's head.

Enraged at this unexpected turn of events, the bear dashed furiously into the forest. Witnesses later saw it roaming through the woods, trying to get rid of the bucket hanging from its neck.

Coming to grips with threatening problems, whether it be the surprise appearance of a hungry bear or the risks of nuclear destruction, is never easy.

But God blesses those who try to overcome evil with good. You may be surprised at how much you can accomplish with His help. Taking a stand, with imagination and daring, is better than doing nothing or succumbing to frustration.

❖

"With the humble is wisdom."
[PROVERBS 11:2]

❖

Grant me the grace and courage, O Holy Spirit, to meet problems bravely, not be defeated by them.

Young People Helped to Face Life

Baseballs, dart games, chess and checker sets were the tools used by former delinquents to help Manhattan's youngsters get a good start in life.

It was part of a program that also included high school dropouts and recent college graduates. The group—24 in all —spent several summer months trying to improve the chances of young gang members to become constructive members of society.

"You'll have to be patient with them," said the group's supervisor, referring to the young people they worked with.

"Mostly we talk about ourselves," commented another, who added that the conversations focused on "facing up to life—recognizing what you can do—recognizing our weaknesses and our responsibilities."

Frequently those who have made mistakes and then corrected their lives are in a strong position to assist others to do the same. By helping one such person, for the love of Our Lord, you may benefit many more.

❖

"If your brother sin, rebuke him; and if he repent forgive him."　　　　　[LUKE 17:3]

❖

Remind me, O Jesus, that the more I do for others, the more I can imitate You.

Calls Police to Catch Rattlesnake

Convinced there was a rattlesnake in her overnight bag, a frightened woman hurled it out of her Los Angeles apartment window onto the sidewalk.

Then she frantically phoned the police, explaining that she just returned from a trip. She had opened her bag, heard the rattle, snapped it shut again and tossed everything out the window—bag, clothes and all.

Two patrolmen warily opened the bag and dumped out its contents. The buzz grew louder and then something bright rolled out. The 2 policemen were suddenly relieved.

One of them turned to the woman and with a smile said: "Lady, you don't have any rattlesnake. What you've got is your electric toothbrush turned on."

It is not always easy to choose between caution and carelessness when one feels threatened by danger. But God gives a special grace to persons who rely on Him for guidance and strength and at the same time show reasonable prudence in protecting themselves and others.

✧

"The Lord is faithful; He will strengthen you and guard you from evil."
[2 THESSALONIANS 3:3]

✧

Grant that I may show good judgment in all that I think, say and do, O Lord.

Earn Your Reputation Honestly

This unusual notice was posted in a restaurant in Switzerland.

"Diners who are tempted to steal silverware, ash trays and other objects belonging to this establishment are asked to do it discreetly. We want to preserve the good reputation of our clientele."

On the subject of reputation, William Shakespeare had this to say:

> "The purest treasure mortal times afford
> Is spotless reputation; that away,
> Men are but guilded loam or painted clay."

The legitimate desire most people have for others' respect must be backed up by a willingness to make the sacrifices involved in keeping that respect.

While insisting on your own right to a decent reputation, recognize as well that other persons have a similar God-given right.

Pay more attention to the services you can perform for others than to enhancing your own reputation and you will have a good name with the Lord.

❖

"For they loved the praise of men more than the praise of God." [JOHN 12:43]

❖

Help me to imitate Your example, O Jesus, in seeking Your Father's will before my own personal advantage.

You Can Be a Peacemaker

Do you know that the word *"peace"* is mentioned 223 times in the Holy Bible?

You would do well to consider from time to time what Sacred Scripture has to say about peace. This reflection may help you to be a force for peace in your home, on the job and in the mainstream of modern life. Here are a few:

1. The Hebrew psalmist pleaded: "Depart from evil, and do good; seek peace, and pursue it." [PSALM 34:14]
2. When Christ was born, the angels sang: "On earth peace among men with whom He is pleased!" [LUKE 2:14]
3. During His Sermon on the Mount, the Master paid a special tribute to those who take the trouble to work for peace: "Blessed are the peacemakers, for they shall be called sons of God." [MATTHEW 5:9]
4. At the Last Supper, Jesus reminded His disciples: "Peace I leave with you, My peace I give to you; not as the world gives do I give to you. Let not your hearts be troubled, neither let them be afraid." [JOHN 14:27]
5. When the Savior rose from the dead, His first words to His Apostles were: "Peace be with you. As the Father has sent Me, even so I send you." [JOHN 20:21]

✧

May I be an instrument of Your peace. O Lord, in every way possible.

Doing Something about It

A television repairman made a dramatic contribution to a Congressional study of highway hazards.

The 49-year-old bachelor kept noticing misplaced road signs, poorly designed freeway access roads and dangerous guardrails in the New York area. And he decided to do something about it.

Armed with a camera, he compiled 700 slides on highway dangers. In 150 of them he showed wrecks that occurred later at the sites of the hazards.

His report brought high praise from Congressmen. "Your layman's-eye-view might well be given urgent attention by our highway engineers and experts," the chairman of the committee commented.

Instead of complaining about problems, small or large, do something to solve them.

You may be happily surprised to see what good can be accomplished as the result of a little initiative on your part.

God blesses those who rise above frustrations and do their bit to change the world for the better.

✧

"And those among the people who are wise shall make many understand."

[DANIEL 11:33]

✧

Inspire me, Holy Spirit, to be a "doer" not merely a "complainer."

Attractive Cruise Offered

Anyone looking for a 60-day cruise in the South Pacific, reasonably light work and pay at the rate of $15,000 a year? Such a dream could have come true for you some time ago —if you happen to be a doctor.

The National Science Foundation in Washington, D.C. advertised in 1965 for a physician to accompany an Antarctic expedition composed of 36 scientists and 48 crew members.

The doctor had to be ready to care for anything from a mild infection to acute appendicitis.

But the foundation assured prospective takers that the passengers were "a generally youthful, vigorous and intelligent group."

Such attractive offers are rare enough to make news. This is an effective reminder that the lives of most of us tend to be more ordinary, and seldom tinged with exotic hues.

But the faithful, unheralded performance of our duties for love of God brings a reward that far surpasses even the attractions of the South Seas.

❖

"Be faithful unto death, and I will give you a crown of life." [REVELATIONS 2:10]

❖

Make me willing to forego some temporal pleasure, Lord, to gain eternity by serving others.

Be the First to Help

Finding a skunk in one's living room can be an unsettling experience. One man in Hamilton, Ontario, found this out when his 6-year-old son awakened him with the unpleasant news.

Dutifully descending the stairs from his bedroom, the father saw for himself the little animal sleeping peacefully behind the sofa. The man's fears grew because the house had just been painted and the living room contained new furniture and wall-to-wall carpet.

Phone calls to local officials and a pest control company produced surprise and amusement—but no results. Finally, the SPCA enticed the skunk into a trap baited with a large chunk of steak. It was then released in the woods some distance away.

When others need help, whether from a furry intruder or from more serious interference, we should be the first, not the last, to try to provide it.

In short, assist others without delay when the love of God calls for it.

✧

"Do all things without grumbling or questioning." [PHILIPPIANS 2:14]

✧

Inspire me with such a generous spirit, O Lord, that I will be ever alert to the needs of others.

Ty Cobb's Secret—He Kept Trying

Practically everyone has heard of Ty Cobb, one of the all-time greats of baseball. But few realize that his stolen-base average was far below that of a nearly unheard-of player named Max Carey.

In his best year, Cobb stole 96 bases and failed 38 times, for a 71 per cent average. Carey stole 51 bases, failed only twice for a 96 per cent average.

Despite his lower average, Cobb is remembered because he achieved twice as much. He was willing to risk failure in order to win.

A familiar saying underlines this point: "Consider the turtle—he doesn't make any progress unless he sticks his neck out."

Millions of people like you are needed to take reasonable chances—and to risk being wrong on occasion—so that others may have the freedom, economic security, education and other God-given rights to which they are entitled.

Otherwise, your own corner may be peaceful for a while, but the very roots of society will wither.

✧

"You have need of endurance, so that you may do the will of God and receive what is promised." [HEBREWS 10:36]

✧

Give me the humility, Jesus, to get up each time I fail in carrying out Your will.

Not as Strong as He Thought

One Dutch couple landed in the hospital when a husband's "strongman" act backfired.

The man was demonstrating his physical prowess by holding his wife by the ankles from their first floor balcony, but she suddenly grew panicky.

The woman reached for a clothesline 12 feet above the ground. The line snapped under her weight and she grabbed for her husband.

The strain proved too much for the man. Both of them fell to the pavement below.

The two were hospitalized, the wife with a concussion and the husband with an injured ankle.

The old adage, "He who tries to prove too much proves nothing," applies today as it always did.

Whether it is a question of your ability in the field of physical, intellectual or moral strength, try to keep within the bounds of your clear limitations.

The Lord will help you to achieve great things for yourself and others, provided you trust in Him for the outcome—and not only in yourself.

✧

"God is our refuge and strength."

[PSALM 46:1]

✧

Let my self-knowledge, O Holy Spirit, be an incentive to realistic action and not foolhardiness.

Cheater Cheats Himself

The head of a large building corporation delegated one of his key men to erect a model house in the most exclusive residential section of the city.

The man was authorized to use only the best material and the most skilled labor. But the great confidence put in him proved to be too much of a temptation.

"No one will ever know what goes into the unseen parts," he said to himself. "Why hire such expensive labor? Why use such costly materials?"

So he began to cut corners by substituting inferior supplies and hiring second-rate workers. He pocketed the difference for himself.

When the job was finally completed, the dream house suddenly became a nightmare. As he started to turn the keys over to the president of his firm, he was stunned when his employer graciously stopped him and said: "No, no, we are giving you this house as a token of our high esteem for your many years of splendid and faithful service."

St. Paul pinpoints the moral in these few words:

✧

"For whatever a man sows, that he will also reap."   [GALATIANS 6:8]

✧

Keep me reminded, O divine Master, that an honest world starts with myself as much as with anyone.

Modern "Surrey with a Fringe on Top"

Thatched roofs will be "the thing" in the automobile of tomorrow if one Englishman's style is adopted.

When John Potter of London bought a used car, he balked at the idea of paying an additional $112 for a new top.

Since he was a thatcher by trade, he decided to utilize his talents.

"A few people raise their eyebrows when they see it," he said. "But why should I worry? It keeps out the rain."

Then he concluded: "It only took a few evenings to do and I must say, it works fine."

Imagination and skill can come up with some surprising results, whether in taking care of one's own needs or in serving the best interests of others.

God intends that you use your talents, be they few or many, in an outgoing, constructive way.

Then the world will be that much better for your being in it.

✧

"... being no hearer that forgets but a doer that acts, he shall be blessed in his doing."
[JAMES 1:25]

✧

Stimulate my imagination, O Lord, and strengthen my resolve to find solutions to human problems.

JUNE 7

How to Regain Your Vigor

Do you have that "chronic-overtired feeling"?

If so, here are 7 suggestions—summarized from Life Extension "Guidelines."

1. Have a complete physical examination. Usually, no more than 1 person in 20 needs treatment.
2. Eliminate unnecessary activities you say you want to do but never get around to. You can lift a burden right there.
3. Do more than complain. If the world's troubles weigh you down, tackle one that you can handle.
4. Avoid loneliness.
5. Plan ahead. Have pleasant events to look forward to.
6. Avoid the fallacy of excessive rest.
7. Take an interest in other people.

We can thank the Lord for making us in such a way that we are happiest when we forget self and go out of our way to show personal concern for others.

Respect the feelings and rights of everyone you can reach and you won't have time to be "overtired."

❖

"Let us not grow weary in well-doing, for in due season we shall reap, if we do not lose heart." [GALATIANS 6:9]

❖

Enlighten me, O Holy Spirit, so that I may see the viewpoint of others and act in their behalf.

168

One-of-a-Kind Wedding Gift

There's one way to be certain that the gift you give a bride will not be returned for something else.

When Stella Peel of Whorlton, England, married Dennis Ardus, an explorer, she found one wedding gift that was not exchangeable.

A mountain peak in the Antarctic had been named "Stella" in honor of her marriage by a group of explorer friends of her husband.

A gift of this kind is a rare tribute. Every bride naturally expects and deserves to be honored on her wedding day.

But she should take care at the same time not to become so preoccupied with the incidentals that she gives scant attention to the tremendous significance of the marriage itself.

Focus primary attention on the unique privilege of husbands and wives in cooperating with the Creator by generating new life and then every gift will take on a holy significance.

✧

"Let marriage be held in honor among all."
[HEBREWS 13:1]

✧

Grant, O Lord, that all married couples will keep ever conscious of the great privilege You entrust to them.

Your Telephone Voice

How is your telephone personality? Every time you make or receive a phone call, your voice reflects the type of person you are.

The New York Telephone Company has prepared several practical pointers on how you can make your phone conversations more effective. Here are a few:

1. Be attentive. The person you are talking with will appreciate it if you listen politely.
2. Say "Please," "Thank you," and "You're welcome."
3. Smile while you are talking. It will be reflected in your voice.
4. Visualize the person you are talking with as an individual. Speak to him, not to the telephone.
5. If your voice is warm and friendly, if you are courteous and tactful, people will enjoy talking to you.

By putting such recommendations into practice, you will be applying to another facet of life the divine standard of showing the same consideration for others that you expect for yourself.

✧

"So whatever you wish that men would do to you, do so to them." [MATTHEW 7:12]

✧

Teach me, O Lord, to speak to others in the same way I wish them to speak to me.

What to Do in a Robbery

One robbery victim learned a lesson in law from the man who relieved her of $100 at knifepoint.

"Go into the back room," he told the dress shop operator, "and wait until I leave. Then call the police."

Startled, the woman exclaimed, "Do I have to call the police?"

He replied simply, "All robberies have to be reported to the police," and walked out.

One could speculate endlessly on this comment. Whether the criminal acted out of whim, humor or a sense of the inevitable, it showed some awareness that his deed would not go unpunished.

While such flagrant violations of law—both civil and moral —are easy to recognize, how often do many of us ponder the consequences of less obvious offenses.

Small dishonesties, denial of equal rights to others or harmful falsehoods may not receive retribution in this life. But there is One Who sees all and eventually rights all wrongs.

✧

"And the measure you give will be the measure you get." [MATTHEW 7:2]

✧

Let me put into life, O Jesus, not merely seek to take out.

To Catch a Monkey

When firemen and pet experts tried to recapture an escaped monkey in Rome, they were baffled on every attempt.

They tried ladders, scare tactics and the temptation of choice monkey food to lure the elusive animal from its perch high in a pine tree. Nothing worked.

"Just no way to reach her," sighed one of her pursuers, who was about to give up.

Then two small boys came by. Without fanfare they quietly climbed the tree and brought the monkey down without a protest. The grown-ups had overlooked the fact that small boys climb trees nearly as well as monkeys.

The resourcefulness of youth is a thing to wonder at. Young people's initiative, unspoiled by cynicism or despair, is both a hope and a responsibility.

Instead of overlooking, or worse, discouraging the ardor of young people, urge them to use their divine spark of greatness for the benefit of all men, not to keep it just to themselves.

❖

"The child grew and became strong, filled with wisdom; and the favor of God was upon Him."   [LUKE 2:40]

❖

Let me live up to my own potential, O Jesus, and help others do the same.

The Bridegroom Was Confused

A bride was stranded at the altar when the would-be groom suddenly departed from the church.

In explaining his action, the 20-year-old man said: "I wasn't scared. It's just that I couldn't bring myself to say 'yes.'"

He continued: "I just wanted to get away . . . I've got the wanderlust in me. I even took my passport to the church because I still had not decided whether I wanted to travel or wanted a wife."

Tearfully, but emphatically, his fiancee said: "He will not get away with it as easily as that. I am contacting my lawyer." Then she added pointedly: "What makes it even worse is that I gave him $7 to buy a new pair of shoes for the wedding."

While unfairness seldom shows itself in such a dramatic way, engaged couples ought to show a loving consideration for the rights and feelings of their prospective partners. They can thus help bring into their wedded lives the mutual peace and understanding the Lord wishes them to enjoy.

✧

"Bring their lives to fulfillment in health and happiness and mercy." [*Tobit* 8:17]

✧

Inspire me, O Savior, to spread a reverence and respect for the holiness of marriage.

Children Are People Too!

Parents can forget that children are as sensitive to public scolding as they themselves would be.

Columnist Dorothy Rose points out that as children grow past the toddler stage they develop an understandable pride and sensitivity. They are humiliated by stinging words, tongue-lashings, or other forms of embarrassment in front of visitors.

"Anything that weakens a youngster's pride in his parents or himself," she warns, "can be harmful to his emotional well-being."

Parents must sometimes make corrections on the spot, no matter who is present. But much more is gained by giving deserved rebukes in private.

Persons in positions of authority are always much more effective if they can combine gentleness and tact with required firmness. They will more readily acquire this divine habit if they realize that they are cooperators with their Father in heaven Who is patiently kind with all His children.

✧

"May the Lord direct your hearts to the love of God and to the steadfastness of Christ."
[2 THESSALONIANS 3:5]

✧

Teach me, O loving Savior, to disagree without becoming disagreeable.

The Barn Came Tumbling Down

The jet age caught up dramatically with a couple living on a farm near Albany, N.Y. But they found it brought mixed blessings.

When a sonic boom set off by a jet airplane flying over their 3-story barn caused it to collapse into a heap of rubble, they didn't mind a bit. They had planned to have it torn down anyway so they were saved the expense.

Their delight was short-lived, however. They discovered to their grief that the barn had fallen right on top of their brand new automobile.

Science has made breathtaking progress in the past few decades. It has brought great benefits to mankind. But its potential for good is often offset by the harm that results from human failure to control the forces that God has placed at our disposal.

Rather than be frightened by the startling developments of our scientific age, take whatever steps you can to see that they always serve man, never dominate or injure him.

✧

"Come, let us walk in the light of the Lord."
[ISAIAH 2:5]

✧

Thanks to You, O bountiful Father, for the countless blessings that You have hidden in nature.

Gratitude Dear to God and Man

A fifth-grade teacher gave her pupils an assignment to write a "letter of appreciation" for a favor or kindness received.

One child's sentiments impressed her so much that she sent the letter to the Buffalo Evening News. Shortly afterwards, the paper ran it in one of its columns.

The message read as follows: "Dear God, thank you for everything that you have given to me. I appreciate your kindness very much. Thank you for my mother, my father, my sister, and my brothers. God, how can I thank you for loving me so much? I am very grateful to you. James McFarland."

Gratitude is a quality dear to both God and man. Take every opportunity to show appreciation to those from whom you have received any benefits. Start in the family circle.

Be grateful also to those at work, in school, in civic affairs and in all key areas.

Gratitude to your fellowman can also be a manner of expressing gratitude to God.

✧

". . . Always and for everything giving thanks in the name of our Lord Jesus Christ to God the Father." [EPHESIANS 5:20]

✧

Thanks to You, O Lord, for all that I am and hope to be.

Something New on the Menu

A hippo sandwich is the latest addition to the menu of tourists in East Africa.

There is a good reason for the sudden availability of this particular dish. The hippopotamus population, it appears, is becoming so large that they are imperiling other wild animals in the region.

Professional hunters were brought into Tanganyika, where the hippopotamus threat is greatest, to shoot 500 of the big animals in an effort to thin out their ranks. Wildlife experts are hoping that hippo meat will prove to be a popular food for everybody.

Hippo sandwiches may not be to everyone's liking but most would agree with the larger goal they are meant to serve—that of restoring the balance of nature.

Conservation of wildlife, of soil, forest, and other natural resources is one way for man to express gratitude to the all-generous Creator who put them there.

Show thanks to Him in an even greater way as well, by respecting each fellow human being as a person made in His holy image.

✧

"Whatever you do, in word or deed, do everything in the name of the Lord Jesus, giving thanks to God the Father through him."
[COLOSSIANS 3:17]

✧

Assist me, O Lord, to appreciate the marvels of Your world by seeking to preserve and develop them.

Use, Don't Abuse

A circus performer who boasted that he could digest anything, complained one day of a stomach ache.

The pains became so acute that doctors ordered an examination. One look at the X-ray was enough to warrant an immediate operation.

The contents of the circus man's stomach astounded even the patient. Among the items extracted were 70 keys, 16 penknives, 36 nails and nuts, plus a quantity of iron and glass.

Though you probably won't swallow such an indigestible menu, there are many ways in which one can neglect to treat the body with the care that the Creator intended for it.

Don't wait until you have nearly lost the blessings of health before appreciating them.

Show a practical concern also for those who are burdened with bodily afflictions and you are more likely to be reasonably solicitous for your own good health.

✦

"There is no wealth better than health of body, and there is no gladness above joy of heart." [SIRACH 30:16]

✦

Thanks to You, O Lord, for the many blessings of body You have entrusted to me.

Colorful Way to Collect the Rent

A red automobile doesn't usually cause any special stir. But that's not the case with one seen occasionally on the streets of Hawarden, England.

When this particular red car stops in front of a house, it is a blushing reminder that the tenant is late in paying his rent.

The tell-tale auto is seldom parked very long outside any house. To avoid prolonging the embarrassing situation in full sight of neighbors, the delinquent occupant of the house generally pays up promptly and without further discussion.

It is not always easy to meet one's legitimate obligations. But, by the same token, we should not wait to be prodded or shamed into fulfilling responsibilities when we are in a position to do so.

The Lord Himself has given us a practical yardstick on which to base both our attitudes and actions towards those to whom we are indebted: show others the same consideration that you would expect for yourself if you were in their position.

✧

"Have the same care for one another."
[1 CORINTHIANS 12:25]

✧

Let me always treat others, O Lord, as if I were the others.

He Knew What He Wanted

One frustrated golfer hit the boiling point after plunking four balls one after another into a stream.

Picking up his bag of clubs, he hurled them into the water, and then did the same with his golf cart. His spiked shoes met the same watery fate.

When bystanders saw him wade into the water a few minutes later, they thought he had had a change of heart. But instead of retrieving his disgarded possessions, he just fumbled for the sunken bag, unzipped a pocket and came up with a set of car keys. Then he purposefully shoved the bag into deeper water.

Learn to keep calm in tense moments and you will be far less inclined to do anything that you may live to regret or that might offend the interests of God, self or others.

Master every temptation to give vent to exasperation, however justified it may seem to you. By doing so, you will be taking a big step in promoting the harmony that the Lord wishes us to enjoy in every facet of life, be it at home, at work or even on the golf course.

❖

"The anger of man does not work the righteousness of God."   [JAMES 1:20]

❖

Grant me the vision, O Lord, to see myself as I really am.

Family's Peril Brings out Best in Father

A young doctor walked 14 miles in sub-zero temperature last winter to get help for his wife and two children trapped by snowdrifts in their car.

The Colorado physician struggled through snow for nine hours, sometimes sinking up to his chin in drifts as he fought his way along.

After vainly trying to free the car, he had left instructions for his wife to keep the engine running until he returned. Reaching a service station, he alerted authorities. A rescue party took him back to his stranded family.

The concern that motivates people when loved ones face danger enables many to perform feats of strength and endurance otherwise unthinkable.

Although we may seldom advert to it, many grave perils threaten the family of man. But there is hope, so long as enough persons like you respond to God's promptings to find lasting solutions to man's family, community, political, economic, racial and other problems.

✧

"Have we not all one Father? Has not one God created us? Why then are we faithless to one another?" [MALACHI 2:10]

✧

Make me aware of human need wherever it exists, Father, and spur me to prompt, effective action.

Late—And Proud of It

The world is always 20 minutes ahead of one 95-year-old man in Coventry, England.

Here is how he explains his contention that everyone is out of step but himself:

"In 1922," he recalled, "the clocks were changed 20 minutes. I never accepted this. Nobody was going to take 20 minutes out of my life."

So he kept his watch set for the old time. He is 20 minutes late for every appointment.

As a result of this persistence, the determined man has been dismissed from a half-dozen jobs for tardiness.

"They won't beat me," he declared. "I'm going to die 20 minutes late to show them I was right."

There is a certain satisfaction—and often much merit—in holding to one's views in spite of opposition.

But when the principle to which one is sticking turns out to be needless or even wrong, then it is time to reconsider.

The Lord expects each of us to make reasonable accommodations to get along with our fellow men.

✧

"Therefore let any one who thinks that he stands take heed lest he fall."
[1 CORINTHIANS 10:12]

✧

Help me to be persevering, O Lord, but not stubborn.

Finishes High School at 56

After three tries, a 56-year-old man finally received his high school diploma.

As a teenager, upon completion of grammar school 40 years ago, he dropped his studies and went to work. But every time he had an opportunity to get a better job, he found that lack of a high school diploma prevented him from improving his position.

The crowning blow was the loss of a job as an attendant in a court on Long Island, when it was classified under Civil Service. He was released because he had not completed his high school studies.

It was then that the disappointed man decided to get his diploma, no matter how much effort it cost. He attended night school but, because he had been so long away from his studies, he failed three times. Instead of giving up, he finally reached his goal and applied for his old job as a court attendant.

Encourage young people to finish their studies and develop the talents God gave them, rather than short-change themselves for life by dropping out of school.

❖

"Listen to advice and accept instruction, that you may gain wisdom for the future."
[PROVERBS 19:20]

❖

Inspire youth, O Holy Spirit, to face responsibilities rather than dodge them.

Surgeon Prays before Operation

Just before he performed a difficult operation, a well-known doctor paused to say a brief prayer.

Afterwards, a visiting friend of his told him he was surprised that he had done this. "I thought a surgeon relied solely on his ability," he said to him.

"A surgeon is only human," came the reply. "He cannot work miracles by himself. I am certain science could not have advanced as far as it has were it not for something far stronger than mere man."

Then he explained: "I feel so close to God when I am operating that I don't know where my skill leaves off and His begins."

The more you realize you are in the divine Presence at all times, the more likely you are to turn to the Lord for guidance and strength, as well as give of your best to the task before you.

True dependence on God will stimulate you to develop and put to practical use the talents He has entrusted to you. You will be more apt to pray as if all depended on God and act as if all depended on yourself.

❖

"How would anything have endured if You had not willed it? Or how would anything not called forth by You have been preserved?"
[WISDOM 11:25]

❖

Enlighten and direct me, O Holy Spirit, in all that I think, say and do.

Profiting by a Jail Sentence

Many prisoners in New Guinea find life in jail so attractive that they must be ordered to return to their villages when their term is completed.

Prison for the inmates means regular food, tobacco, shelter, entertainment, learning a trade and acquiring a basic education.

Naturally, the relative security of jail life is more appealing to the convicts than the primitive conditions of the village.

But prison officials have had more in mind than the personal comfort of their wards. They make the jail term a time for rehabilitation as well as for punishment and correction. The result is that prisoners return to their villages as assets rather than liabilities. Many join with the leaders of their tribe, and even sometimes become the head man.

Do what you can to see that in addition to restraining what is evil in man, you bring out the potential for good that God entrusts to every human being He sends into the world.

✧

"It is my prayer that your love may abound more and more, with knowledge and all discernment so that you may approve what is excellent." [PHILIPPIANS 1:9]

✧

Inspire me, O Holy Spirit, to find good in even the worst of men.

Too Many Sea Shells

A request for "a few sea shells" brought a ton and a half of them to a startled London man.

Wanting the shells to decorate his apartment, the 24-year-old Englishman wrote a letter to a Zanzibar firm. He expected to receive a small box in return. But to his amazement, he was stunned by 2,912 pounds of shells packed in 10 sacks, nine cases and two barrels—and a freight bill for $308.

The distressed man's story was widely printed in newspapers. Offers to buy the shells began to pour in, and the entire shipment was soon sold to a collector for a price at a slight profit.

Consciously, or not, any of us may run the risk of accumulating an abundance of material things for which we have little need. To keep properly detached, it is important that we ask ourselves: "How much is enough?"

God will help you if you respond to the spiritual and physical needs of others with the same imagination and zest with which you pursue your own.

✧

"Seek first His kingdom and His righteousness, and all these things shall be yours as well." [MATTHEW 6:33]

✧

Give us neither too little nor too much, O Lord.

Boy Obeys Orders, but . . .

An 11-year-old found himself hanging from a manned balloon, 3,000 feet over the California countryside.

It all started when Danny Nowell went over to look at a hot-air balloon which was being kept in place by 6 other people holding ropes.

"Grab a rope," someone yelled. He did so but when everyone else let go, he held on.

When the pilot heard cries for help, he began "spilling air" and descended 25 feet a second.

Danny finally landed in a tree, 3 miles from the take-off point. Although suffering from shock and a few bruises, he was declared in good shape.

Obedience is a good thing, but we have to weigh: 1) who is giving the orders; 2) whether they are reasonable; and 3) if there are any special circumstances.

Common sense is a trait that should grow with each passing year. The Lord will enable us to make wise choices in the future if we use our judgment to the best of our ability.

✧

"Happy is the man who finds wisdom, and the man who gets understanding."

[PROVERBS 3:13]

✧

Enlighten me, O Holy Spirit, to know what is right and grant me the strength to do it.

As They See Us

Some years ago a young businessman who had risen to a position of importance fell in love with a well-known and highly respected actress. For many months he was constantly in her company, escorting her to all "the right places." Eventually he decided to marry the young lady.

Before doing so, however, he hired a private detective to investigate her. The task was assigned to a special agent, who had no knowledge of the identity of his client.

Finally the agent's report was sent to him. It read: "Miss —— has an excellent reputation. Her past is spotless, her associates beyond reproach. The only hint of scandal is that in recent months she has been seen in the company of a businessman of doubtful reputation."

There is a tendency in most of us to assume that we are just a little bit better than others.

If we try to see ourselves as others see us, and especially as God sees us, perhaps we would have a less exalted opinion of ourselves.

✧

"Why do you see the speck that is in your brother's eye, but do not notice the log that is in your own eye?" [LUKE 6:41]

✧

O Lord, grant me the grace always to see the good in others and the faults in myself.

188

Hospitality Seeks No Reward

Do you know the definition of the word "hospitality"?

The dictionary defines it as "the spirit, practice, or act of receiving and entertaining strangers and guests without reward and with kindness and consideration."

The word comes from the Latin *"hospes,"* meaning "guest."

Notice that the dictionary includes entertaining as well as receiving guests; that is, welcoming them with heartfelt kindness as well as providing them with a roof and something to eat.

The very meaning of hospitality excludes the idea of expecting any material compensation. It is a free gift, given out of the goodness of one's heart, expecting nothing in return.

"Where there is room in the heart, there is room in the house," runs a Danish proverb.

"Be bright and jovial among your guests." (Shakespeare)

Give thought today to the ancient saying, "When a guest comes to visit you, it is Christ Who comes."

✧

"I was hungry and you gave Me food, I was thirsty and you gave Me drink, I was a stranger and you welcomed Me." [MATTHEW 25:35]

✧

Grant me the largeness of heart, O Jesus, to be open and kindly in hospitality, especially to those who need it.

Stillborn Baby Wins Fight for Life

Just 11 hours after a baby was born apparently dead, it showed signs of life in its tiny coffin.

Doctors in Hirson, France, declared: "Without any doubt, the baby was clinically stillborn." All efforts at resuscitation, drug injections, heart massage and oxygen had produced no response.

The next morning, as a hospital attendant prepared to transfer the lifeless infant to the funeral home, one of its arms began to move.

The child was quickly given oxygen and moved to a larger hospital. The overjoyed father told the funeral parlor to cancel everything.

Three months later the child was taken from the incubator and returned to its parents.

The birth of a baby is such an oft-repeated occurrence that we may fail to recognize it for the wondrous act of God's loving providence that it is.

The birth of a child, the return of spring, the rising of the sun—all these testify to the divine promise of final resurrection of us all.

✧

"I am the resurrection and the life."

[JOHN 11:25]

✧

Fill me with trust in Your goodness, O Lord,
in spite of apathy, hardship and opposition.

One Driver Causes 35 Crashes

A massive pileup of 35 automobiles on a fog-bound freeway near San Diego, Calif., caused the death of two motorists and injury to 34 others.

The giant mishap was triggered when one driver suddenly slowed down while passing a traffic accident. Other motorists following him at high speed could not see through the fog in time. In a chain reaction of screeching tires, tortured metal and breaking glass one car slammed into another.

Witnesses testified they could hear cars crashing. Some even turned upside down. The freeway was jammed for hundreds of yards. Screams for help from the injured caught in the tangled wreckage were heard on all sides.

It is seldom easy to foresee the far-reaching consequences of what one person does—or fails to do. All the more reason that we should keep ever alert.

If we are motivated by a deep concern for the God-given rights of our fellow men, we will think, pray, talk, act—and drive, too—with that in mind.

✧

"Let all that you do be done in love."
[1 CORINTHIANS 16:14]

✧

Enlighten me, O Holy Spirit, so that I prevent trouble for others as well as for myself.

Littering Is a Costly Business

Litterbugs cost the United States 100 times as much as all reported bank robberies and burglaries.

This startling fact was disclosed in research done by Keep America Beautiful, Inc.

In one recent year, $4.5 million was stolen in all bank robberies and burglaries made known to police. During the same period $500 million went towards picking up litter strewn on highways, in streets and in parks.

Each act of carelessness adds to the ever-mounting price that all must pay to restore our countryside to something of its original beauty.

Likewise, thoughtlessness in more serious matters undermines the peace and prosperity of everyone.

Every effort by citizens to uphold standards of integrity in government, business, labor and community life contributes to building up the common good.

Do all in your power, with trust in the Lord, to take your stand for what is right in small matters and large.

✧

"By the blessing of the upright a city is exalted." [PROVERBS 11:11]

✧

Keep me aware of my personal responsibility, Lord, in both public and private affairs.

It Was a Wolf after All

When a woman "cried wolf" in Claygate, England, no one believed her; not until they saw the wolf for themselves. It had escaped from a nearby zoo.

The lady happened to be walking in the woods when a shaggy animal started to pester her dog, Laddie. When she tried to shoo the intruder away, she suddenly saw fierce eyes and vicious teeth turned in her direction. Then the awful truth dawned on her.

The frightened woman dashed off, followed by her dog, followed by the wolf.

Reaching home she saw 2 men sitting in a car. They laughed at her when she shouted "wolf," but quickly changed their minds when they saw the real thing. One man grabbed a garden pitchfork and sent the wolf scampering away.

Rather than laugh off the slightest warnings that involve the physical or spiritual well-being of yourself or others, take a few moments to check on the facts.

God expects you to avoid the extremes of being over-cautious on the one hand or too careless on the other.

❖

"In the shadow of Your wings I will take refuge, till the storms of destruction pass by."
[PSALM 57:1]

❖

Grant, O Lord, that I may always seek the truth, not ignore it.

193

Silent Duel Causes Needless Harm

A mailman on a bicycle and a motorist fought it out without a word being spoken.

As a crowd looked on, the driver honked his horn at the rider who blocked his way at a stoplight.

After the auto nudged forward and overturned the bike and rider, the cyclist got up and kicked in both headlights of the car.

Then the driver bashed the spokes of his opponent's vehicle, only to have his own foglight broken.

In retaliation, the motorist lifted the bike and dashed it to the ground. The mailman thrust his tire pump through the windshield of the car.

As the motorist drove off, his foe kicked a dent in the door of the auto.

Stubbornness and lack of communication seldom causes such openly destructive damage. But just as hostility begets hostility, so Christlike love eventually melts the hardest of hearts.

If you answer hardness with gentleness, you will gain the reward God has reserved for peacemakers.

✧

"Blessed are the peacemakers, for they shall be called sons of God."   [MATTHEW 5:9]

✧

Give me the strength and courage, O gentle Master, to be Your follower in fact as well as in name.

Keep This a Nation under God

In 1751, twenty-five years before the signing of the Declaration of Independence, the Founding Fathers sent an order to England for the now-famous Liberty Bell. They specified that the following passage from the Holy Bible be inscribed on it:

"Proclaim liberty throughout all the land unto
all the inhabitants thereof." [LEVITICUS 25:10]

Keep in the forefront of American life the sublime concept on which our freedom depends—that we derive our rights from God, not from the State.

You can do a service by helping to keep everyone aware that the purpose of government is to protect the God-given rights of each person.

The Declaration of Independence states explicitly: ". . . that all men are created equal, that they are endowed by their Creator with certain unalienable rights."

Do your part by prayer, word and deed to keep your country, in Abraham Lincoln's reverent phrase, "this nation under God."

❖

"Unless the Lord watches over the city, the
watchman stays awake in vain."

[PSALM 127:1]

❖

Keep us mindful, O Lord, that we derive our rights from You and that the purpose of government is to protect our God-given rights.

Banker's Faith Pays Off

Good business sense, honesty and a faith in people were turned into a winning combination by one bank manager who opened a new branch in the run-down part of an eastern city.

Despite some skeptics, he prepared the way by speaking to individuals and groups in the area concerning the advantages of good banking services.

Now everybody is glad he did. The residents of the predominantly Negro area, often burdened by high interest rates, found him fair and helpful.

"I found one man paying $196 a month to 11 different places," he said. "By consolidating the debt he was able to reduce monthly payments to $93.

"If people would only treat people as people," he commented, "we'd be a lot better off."

The Lord expects you to show reasonable confidence in the ability and good will of everyone.

By considering each person on his merits—and not making unfair generalizations—you do your part to build up the community, nation and world.

✧

"Always seek to do good to one another and to all."　　　　　[1 THESSALONIANS 5:15]

✧

Let me see every man, O Jesus, as a brother for whom You gave Your life.

For 6 Jugs of Water

Twelve miles over hot, dusty fields is the journey that residents of Deenadag, a tiny village in India's Bihar State, must make for six jugs of water.

Carrying one jug on her head and another on her hip, a village girl begins her first of three trips at daybreak to a nearly dry river bed two miles from her village. Because it is early, the temperature is only 105 degrees. Later, it will rise to 115.

At least four villages in Bihar reached the same extremity during the recent drought. Government tank trucks bring water each morning to each village. This, supplemented by treks to the river bed, has managed to keep the villagers and their cattle alive.

It is difficult for most of us who have ample supplies of water even to imagine this.

But it is important that we become aware of such problems and then do something about them in the Lord's name. Countless millions of persons suffer from lack of such basic needs as adequate food, water, housing, medical care and attention. They are all our brothers.

✧

"Let justice roll down like waters, and right-eousness like an everflowing stream."

[AMOS 5:24]

✧

Teach me, O Savior, what I can do to help solve some of the problems that beset mankind.

Easy Job Attracts College Graduate

An Oxford graduate feels that a railway porter's job is the most satisfactory occupation for him.

The young man, 23, flabbergasted his friends when he said he had found his "niche in life" by taking a $36-a-week job as a porter at a small railway station.

In fact, he was enthusiastic about the advantages of his job.

"It's a wonderful uncomplicated life," he said. "You can have a good sit-down whenever you feel like it."

To be sure, the better educated a person is, the better fitted he should be for any station in life, however inconspicuous it may seem.

But the advantages of learning are accompanied by many responsibilities. They are entrusted to us by God on condition we use them in a manner that will benefit others as well as self.

You are more apt to increase your knowledge as the years go on if you seek to enrich the lives of other people.

✥

"Everyone to whom much is given, of him will much be required." [LUKE 12:48]

✥

Thanks to You, O generous Master, for the blessings of knowledge.

Small Oversight Wrecks Plane

A private pilot crash landed in his small rented airplane at Kennedy International Airport in New York not long ago.

The single-engine plane slid 350 feet on its belly down the concrete runway as the uninjured man climbed out of the damaged craft. He frankly explained to puzzled onlookers: "I just forgot to lower the wheels."

Little things often mean the difference between safety and tragedy—between life and death.

People who are negligent in matters that seem to be of minor significance often find that they are defeating their chances of achieving the bigger goals they would like to reach.

You have countless opportunities to make constructive efforts on a small scale and thus prepare the way for the success that counts for both time and eternity.

Yes, take care of the little things, and you will find that the bigger ones are easier to handle.

✧

"You have been faithful over a little, I will set you over much; enter into the joy of your master." [MATTHEW 25:21]

✧

Teach me, O Savior, to see the value of trifles.

Round the World on One Leg

A former Paris tailor is walking around the world on one leg and an artificial limb.

In Turkey, recently, having walked his way through 14 countries, he told interviewers: "I love walking and do not consider myself handicapped having only one leg."

From Turkey, the adventurous man, a 62-year-old bachelor, intends to walk to Iran, India and the Far East and go to the U.S. by ship.

He had become bored as a tailor and then won several walking races in France. Newspapers praised him as "the man who challenges his disability."

"I don't know when I shall complete the world tour," the one-legged man concluded. "All I know is that I want to walk until I die."

Persons with big objectives usually push on despite handicaps that would dishearten most people.

Set your sights on heaven and you will more easily overcome the trials and temptations that beset people who have no goal in life.

✧

"I press on toward the goal for the prize of the upward call of God in Christ Jesus."

[PHILIPPIANS 3:14]

✧

Keep me conscious, O Holy Spirit, of why I am here, where I came from and where I am going.

A Soggy Night's Sleep

Police spent 2 fruitless hours combing the Hudson River for a man who had fallen into the water only to doze off again safely in a drainpipe.

The 35-year-old vagrant's adventure began on a water-front pier where he was sleeping peacefully. When he rolled over too far and plummeted into the river, his companions notified authorities.

A police launch cast about for him through the night until they discovered him in his new resting place. He said that he was awakened by his plunge just long enough to swim over to the drainage pipe and resume his interrupted slumber.

Cervantes in 1615 referred to sleep as "food for the hungry, drink for the thirsty, heat for the cold and cold for the hot."

There is a time and a place for everything but our own need for rest should never interfere with the God-given rights of others or cause inconvenience.

Consider the effects of your actions and there is more chance you will help others, not hurt them.

✧

"So, whether you eat or drink, or whatever you do, do all to the glory of God."
[1 CORINTHIANS 10:31]

✧

Protect me, O Lord, from a preoccupation with my own comfort and make me more attentive to my neighbor.

Act of Kindness Saves Four

An act of hospitality saved 4 lives as the Vaiont dam burst over a small town in Italy and claimed 2,000 victims.

An 87-year-old woman asked her grand-nephew and his family from America to remain with her a few minutes and share a bottle of wine. As a result, they were inside the thick-walled house when the waters came.

The roof collapsed in the wake of the flood, killing the elderly woman, but the sturdy walls of her house protected the 4 others.

The visitors were hospitalized for serious injuries but eventually recovered.

Seldom does a passing kindness make itself felt with such immediacy or with such beneficial effect.

Nevertheless, anyone who reaches out to help another can have far-reaching benefits both in this life and the next.

And even when the results are not evident, you have the satisfaction of knowing that no kindness will be forgotten in the Lord's sight.

✧

"Kindness is like a garden of blessings."
[SIRACH 40:17]

✧

Never let me fail others, O Jesus, when I can
be of real help to them.

An Honest Man by Any Other Name . . . . .

A man known as "Big Bad John" turned out to be a lot better than his nickname implied.

As a motorist got out of a car in Tampa, Fla., a wallet with $18,000 in cash slipped out of his pocket.

A few minutes later, a husky passerby scooped up the money-laden wallet and hurried after the owner.

When offered a reward, the stranger would have none of it. "Maybe you can do something for me someday," he said. To the question of his name, he responded: "Some of my friends call me 'Big Bad John.'"

Those friends might have been amused, surprised or even disbelieving, had they heard of his action. But like most people, there was more to the man with the uncomplimentary nickname than met the eye.

You may never know the full extent of the capabilities for good with which the Lord has endowed you, until "the chips are down."

While resisting the tendency to sell yourself short, go a step further and show a reasonable trust in others.

✧

"Let each of us please his neighbor for his good." [ROMANS 15:2]

✧

Give me ability, O Almighty Father, to bring out the best in others.

The Challenge of Lonely Isolation

Loneliness can affect the brain of human beings or animals if they are isolated for a long period of time.

Tests were made on rodents because they naturally live in groups. By isolating them for a month or more, scientists noted cumulative changes in their body chemistry that could in turn have profound effects on the brain.

The findings can be used for better understanding of the mental condition of astronauts who will be subjected to lengthy periods of loneliness in space as well as the mood behavior in humans.

Persons who are compelled by circumstances to lead lonely lives should constantly strive to reach out to others through prayer, word and deed. Nothing can imprison the spirit of the individual whose heart is filled with love of God and his fellow man.

If loneliness comes your way, then see in it both a challenge and an opportunity to strengthen your kinship with the Lord and mankind. Then you will profit, rather than suffer, from its effects.

✧

"I am not alone, for the Father is with Me."
[JOHN 16:31]

✧

Let me always remember, O Jesus, that in my loneliest moments You are always near.

Ethiopians Struggle for Health

A relentless battle against disease is being waged by Emperor Haile Selassie on behalf of his poverty-stricken people.

A second 5-year plan of the Ethiopian government is giving high priority to public health. Preventive medicines are being stressed.

Malaria, a national scourge, is being combatted with DDT. Leprosy clinics and tuberculosis centers are to be erected in various provinces.

The monarch, while doing all in his power to overcome ignorance, hunger and disease among his people, insists that these scourges can only be completely eradicated by the pooling of the world's resources for peace.

It is both the privilege and responsibility of those who enjoy prosperity to: 1) comprehend the plight of those who don't, and 2) take steps to bring about lasting solutions. Show your gratitude to God for the blessings of body and soul that are yours by working in behalf of those who are deprived of the necessities of life.

✧

"For the needy shall not always be forgotten, and the hope of the poor shall not perish for ever." [PSALM 9:18]

✧

Grant me wisdom and courage, O Jesus, to help those who cannot help themselves.

Spends Half Century Looking for Sister

After searching for his sister for 50 years, a man finally found her living in a neighboring city in California.

Half a century before the brother left Boswell, Oklahoma, at the age of 21 to take a job in Tennessee.

Later his sister moved and he lost track of her. Although each tried repeatedly to locate the other, they did not succeed.

Meanwhile each took separate paths to California. For the past 15 years, without realizing it, they lived only 200 miles apart, the brother in Modesto and the sister in Bakersfield.

Blood relations are drawn together throughout their lives, no matter what distance or circumstances may separate them.

The kinship that binds all human beings together as children of one Father in heaven is even deeper and more powerful. But much remains to be done if mankind is to appreciate the tremendous value of the brotherhood of man under the Fatherhood of God.

✧

"See what love the Father has given us, that we should be called children of God."

[1 JOHN 3:1]

✧

Let me treat all people, O Father, as Your children and my brothers and sisters.

Safety Man at Coney Island

How would you like to ride a roller coaster for a living?

One Coney Island employee has been doing this for 25 years and is none the worse for wear.

Each year from March through September, the 67-year-old Brooklyn man checks the "Cyclone," the "Thunderbolt," the "Caterpillar" and other amusement park rides for safety hazards.

"I can hear a matchstick click on a roller coaster track. It's a sixth sense," he said off-handedly.

When someone asked if his job ever made him dizzy he replied: "No. I can do the whole works in one day."

Few among the thousands of daily riders on the roller coaster ever give a thought to the fact that their safety depends in large part on the skill and attention to detail of a single man.

All persons whose duty it is to ensure the safety and welfare of the public render a valuable service to the common good of all. God will bless your efforts to appreciate and cooperate with what they do.

✧

"Test everything; hold fast what is good."
[1 THESSALONIANS 5:21]

✧

Let me show gratitude, O Lord, for the benefits You send my way through others.

He Didn't Like Shopping Centers

Smashing plate glass windows was one man's way of letting off steam in Littleton, Colorado.

After he had thrown soft drink bottles, one after another, through 10 store windows in a shopping center, police arrested the 46-year-old mischief-maker as he walked along the street.

A patrolman who tried to find out the reason for the man's strange conduct didn't get very far. His only comment was: "I don't like shopping centers."

It is dangerous to allow grudges to build up in oneself. All too often the pent-up spite or rancor explodes in a senseless way, causing widespread harm.

Do more than try to protect yourself against the corrosive effects of sullen hostility on yourself and its damaging results for others.

Fill your heart so full of love of God and all people that your energies will be devoted to strengthen the real or imagined weaknesses of others rather than in allowing resentment for them to take over.

✧

"Love your enemies, do good to those who hate you, bless those who curse you, pray for those who abuse you."   [LUKE 6:27]

✧

Let me learn to put love where there is no love, O Lord.

Show a Creative Touch

Paper clips can boost creative thinking. One airline company found this out to its gratification.

The firm distributes a few simple materials to its executives, telling them to come back in 5 days with their handiwork. The supplies include 6 paper clips, 2 common pins, a block of wood, 3 rubber bands, a piece of white paper, 3 thumb tacks and 2 tongue depressors.

The officials have fashioned such items as miniature helicopters, windmills, sedan chairs, covered wagons and even an ancient Roman catapult.

God gives us the materials for our life—those easy to handle as well as the difficult. He not only enables us to put them to good use but He also provides us with freedom to make of them what we will.

Contradictions and setbacks must be faced along with the joys of achievement.

As long as you persevere, you may be happily surprised at how readily you can fashion the raw materials of life for the good of yourself and others.

✧

"Rejoice before the Lord your God in all that you undertake."   [DEUTERONOMY 12:18]

✧

Help me to be imaginative, O Lord, in the matters that really count.

Wives Enjoy Men's Ease

Housewives enjoy a "day off" at least once a year in a small Greek village.

Adhering to an old custom, the women turn over all household duties to their husbands while they take it easy. They spend the day in local cafés drinking coffee, voicing their opinions on home, family and community, and in general enjoying themselves.

Meanwhile, the husbands are relegated to dusting, scrubbing, polishing, cooking, washing, housecleaning and mending, and to feeding, dressing and minding the children. Any married man caught on the streets is soaked with water and sent back to his kitchen.

This annual experience does much to remind husbands of the never-ending and seldom fully appreciated service their wives render.

In God's plan, both husbands and wives must play their own important roles in making a happy home. The more each appreciates the contribution of the other, the better for the family and the world.

✧

"A good wife is the crown of her husband."
[PROVERBS 12:4]

✧

Inspire all husbands and wives, O Lord, to show their love and appreciation for each other.

Hitchhiker Wins Big Reward

A young man hitchhiked from the Arctic to the lower tip of Africa in 60 days in order to win a $2,800 wager.

The 22-year-old Dutchman maintained he could cover the distance in that time. A Swede said he could not and backed up his challenge with a promise to pay the young adventurer $2,800 if he completed the long trip within the 2-month period.

The conditions included leaving Hammerfest, Sweden, north of the Arctic Circle, without money, following a set route and then sending a cablegram from Cape Point, South Africa, before 10 A.M. of his 60th day out.

The determined hitchhiker reached his faraway destination just in the nick of time. He was able to dispatch a cable to his challenger a mere 45 minutes before the deadline.

People who set big goals for themselves are usually surprised by what they can achieve.

Aim high and you will find that, with God's help, you can reach many heights, including heaven itself.

✧

"Train yourself in godliness . . . as it holds promise for the present life and also for the life to come."   [1 TIMOTHY 4:7]

✧

Grant me the vision and determination, O heavenly Father, to pursue great goals for Your sake.

Heroism in a Flaming Restaurant

A heroic employee died in her attempts to save patrons from a blazing penthouse restaurant in Birmingham, Alabama.

The woman called the fire department when she spotted wisps of smoke coming from the cloakroom. Then, as sheets of flame roared out into the dining area, she led one group to safety.

A cook, seeing her, pleaded with her to come away, but the hostess replied: "No, I've got to help these people get out of here."

Trapped by flames, the hostess was unable to lead the second group to the street before she died.

Few of us are called upon to give our lives in going to the assistance of others in distress.

But in many less spectacular ways we are constantly being summoned to assist people in difficulty.

Our readiness to listen attentively, to give honest advice or to inconvenience ourselves for our fellow man means that God can work through us to the benefit of all.

✧

"Greater love has no man than this, that a man lay down his life for his friends."
[JOHN 15:13]

✧

Make us quick to spot the needs of others, Lord, and unhesitating to go to their assistance.

Simple Solution for Cow's Dilemma

If you had a cow and it fell into a well, how would you get it out?

This was the problem faced by a farmer near Auburn, N.Y., when his 900-pound animal tumbled into a wide-mouthed 15-foot cistern.

The cow was unhurt and more muddy than anything else because there were only a few inches of water at the bottom.

Rather than risk injuring the cow by using a derrick, volunteer firemen decided to pump the well full of water and let Bossie float to safety. It worked.

Problems, big and small, can at times be solved by rather simple solutions that any of us can overlook.

It is important for each of us to do some head-work before we do the footwork.

The Lord has given you a mind and will to help you find solutions for the difficulties that beset others as well as yourself. Ask Him for guidance and you may find that some things are not as insoluble as they at first appear.

✧

"Discretion will watch over you; understanding will guard you."   [PROVERBS 2:11]

✧

Remind me, O Holy Spirit, to stop and reflect before plunging into action.

An Exception to the Rule

Strangely enough, disobeying orders made a hero out of a 12-year-old boy in Globe, Arizona.

He was under strict instructions from his parents to stay out of the water because of a head cold. But when he saw a 5-year-old girl being carried away by the swift current in a nearby creek, he jumped in to help the child.

After both of them were carried 150 feet downstream he finally succeeded in helping her make it to shore.

"Boy, I'll get it when I get home," he told the police. "I've got a cold and wasn't supposed to get wet."

Not all conflicts between a general rule and its exception are as clear-cut as this one. Often it takes great insight, balance and a high sense of purpose to know where to draw the line.

While charity and justice do not always oblige us to prefer the good of others to our own, the true follower of the Lord will ever be ready to do so, should the situation require it.

✧

"And above all these put on love, which binds everything together in perfect harmony."
[COLOSSIANS 3:14]

✧

Make me sensitive to the needs of others, O Holy Spirit, so that I may never miss a chance to be of service.

Death Cheated Twice in a Few Minutes

Two narrow brushes with death within a few minutes left a 58-year-old man from Painesville, Ohio, pretty badly shaken but unhurt.

When he tried to stop for blinker lights at a railroad crossing, his car skidded into the path of the oncoming freight train. The locomotive struck at such an angle that his auto was flipped onto an adjacent track. He thought he was spared.

But his new resting place was far from safe. To his horror, he discovered that now he was in the path of a train coming from the opposite direction. He jumped clear just before his car was demolished.

"It was enough to turn a man's hair gray," he later told friends.

Narrow escapes, whether they happen to others or to ourselves, are like so many sharp barbs reminding us that our earthly life will not last forever.

You needn't worry about your last day if you spend today conscientiously in the sight of God.

Take care of "now" and "later" will take care of itself.

✧

"Why, even the hairs of your head are all numbered." [LUKE 12:7]

✧

Remind me, O Holy Spirit, that my life is in your keeping and help me remind others of the same thing.

Weather Affects Our Personalities

The phrase "under the weather" is more than a figure of speech, according to scientific studies of climatic conditions.

Recent research shows a close link between the weather and how we feel emotionally and physically. Here are some findings:

- Hot, muggy weather makes people depressed.
- Low barometric pressures cause restlessness and inability to concentrate.
- Cold, dry weather steps up mental processes.
- Physical work is best done at about 64 degrees.
- Fog decreases mental efficiency. (One London bank locks up important files on foggy days and restricts its clerks to routine chores.)
- Men are affected by weather extremes more than women.

The very knowledge that outside factors can affect our state of mind can enable us, with God's help, to overcome "the blues."

It should also spur us to cheer up others.

✧

"A cheerful heart is a good medicine."
[PROVERBS 17:22]

✧

Let me recognize my limitations, Lord, and strive to live up to the best that is in me.

216

How to Escape from a Sunken Car

If your automobile should ever take a sudden dive into the water, these tips may save your life.

They were given recently by Mr. J. M. Leeming of the British Columbia Automobile Association.

When the car is sinking, he said, and "you cannot escape through a window, don't panic. Close all the windows and wait for the air pocket to form."

He added: "Before you attempt to open a door or window, wait until the car almost fills with water. During this time keep your head in the air pocket.

"Provided there is no structural damage, the doors should open easily once the water pressure has been equalized. Make your escape through a door or window. To prevent possible internal injury at this point, take a deep breath in the air pocket and exhale slowly during your ascent."

God expects you to take reasonable precautions in protecting yourself—body and soul. Show a similar concern for the well-being of others and you will add a new dimension to your life.

✧

"He who pursues righteousness and kindness will find life and honor." [PROVERBS 21:21]

✧

Enlighten me, O Holy Spirit, on what I should do to live with greater purpose while living longer.

Teenagers Aid the Aged

The boredom of youth and loneliness of age are teaming up to form a winning combination, thanks to a 24-year-old London lawyer.

He and a group of friends have spent more than 5 years enlisting teenagers from the city's youth centers to help old people.

Besides visiting pensioners, they also run various errands for those unable to get about easily.

As a result, 2,000 teenagers in the London area are carrying out such tasks under the direction of 8 counselors, all of whom are in their twenties.

The founder of the operation explained that it began with his conviction that youth—all youth—wants to serve. It just needs to be shown how.

The more an individual is powered by a love of man for the love of God, the more will he find ways of his own to bring human problems closer to solution.

Instead of saying "It can't be done," ask the Lord for help—and then set about to find answers to pressing needs in your own community, nation and world.

✧

"The Son of man came not to be served but to serve." [MATTHEW 20:28]

✧

Teach me, O Holy Spirit, how to find workable solutions for the problems of mankind.

No Taste for Gasoline

Water from his well was making a man in Salem, Ill., so sick that he had to stop drinking it.

It took only a little probing by experts to discover the source of the trouble. Gasoline from a leaky underground tank was seeping into the 18-foot well and polluting the water.

The owner said that things had become so bad that "if you stick your head in the well, it would knock you over." As an experiment he soaked a brick with water from the well and placed it on a stove. It burned with a clear blue flame.

There's little likelihood that your drinking water will be contaminated by gasoline without your realizing it. But poisons of various types can subtly seep their way into both your body and soul without your realizing the damage that is taking place.

Keep alert to the dangers that may undermine—even destroy—persons, families, communities and nations.

God will give you all the assistance you need in this holy task.

✧

"Do you not know that a little leaven leavens the whole lump?" [1 CORINTHIANS 5:6]

✧

Protect me, O Jesus, against the dangers I do not see.

Taxes Bother Little Boy

A little boy wanted to get the "inside story" on taxation so he wrote a letter to the governor of his state of Kansas.

His brief message read as follows: "Dear Governor: How are you? I am fine. I don't know why we have taxes. Will you please tell me?"

In his reply, Gov. John Anderson wrote: "We have taxes so you have a public school to attend, roads for you to travel places, pay a policeman to protect you, courts so you can get fair treatment and protect your rights, and many other things."

Then the governor concluded: "You will probably have to pay taxes all your adult life. Let us hope the money is used honestly and for good purposes."

Do more than "hope" that your taxes are spent wisely. Take steps to see that they are.

With the blessing of freedom entrusted to each of us by God goes the obligation to live up to our personal civic duties, which involve much more than paying taxes.

✦

"Render therefore to Caesar the things that are Caesar's and to God the things that are God's." [MATTHEW 22:21]

✦

Thanks, O Jesus, for the privilege of freedom. May I protect and strengthen it.

Are You Worth Your Salt?

Do you know the origin of the word "salary"?

It comes from the Latin *"sal"* meaning "salt," and dates back many centuries. Roman soldiers were paid a sum of money to enable them to purchase salt or were given an allowance of salt instead of wages.

Salt, being essential to health, was considered a valuable commodity. It was highly taxed and occasionally used in place of cash.

The expression "You're not worth your salt," therefore, has a deeper meaning than most people realize. In effect, it signifies that a person is not actually earning the salary paid him.

You are entitled to a just wage when you work for an employer. But by the same token you are bound in justice to give a dollar's worth of service for every dollar you receive in wages. Failure to do this is to take money that really doesn't belong to you.

In every way show that you are "worth your salt," and you will glorify God, be true to yourself and act fairly towards others.

✧

"You are the salt of the earth; but if salt has lost its taste, how shall its saltiness be restored?" [MATTHEW 5:13]

✧

Let me show the same sense of justice towards others, O Lord, that I expect for myself.

Wins Her After 42 Years

A suitor in Wales who was rebuffed for 42 years finally won his "lady fair." The couple, both 74, recently became "Mr. and Mrs."

For more than 40 years, the persistent, but rather shy man slipped a weekly love letter under his neighbor's door. But she continually refused to speak and mend the spat that had parted them many years before.

After writing 2,184 love letters without ever getting a spoken or written answer, the single-hearted old man eventually summoned up enough courage to present himself in person. He knocked on the door of the reluctant lady and asked for her hand.

To his delight and surprise, she accepted. Perseverance can achieve wonders. Far more people would gain their objective if they were willing to endure the patient plodding that is the usual price of any worthwhile victory.

In pursuing your heart's desire, whether it be the legitimate joys of this life or the everlasting ones of heaven, keep pushing on when you are tempted to falter.

✧

"If we endure, we shall also reign with Him."
[2 TIMOTHY 2:12]

✧

Grant, O Father, that I may have the stick-to-it-iveness needed to win the battle of life.

Homemade Sodas on Tap

Two teenagers had the time of their lives when hot and cold seltzer water started flowing from the faucets of their Newark, N.J. apartment house.

Over a period of several days, homemade sodas were at their disposal at the flick of a wrist, until the mystery was cleared up.

The cause of the unusual occurrence was a defective valve and pressure gauge on a carbonator at a nearby soda fountain. The carbonic acid somehow entered the pipes of the apartment house and caused the unusual effects.

"It was fun while it lasted," the teenagers sighed.

Young people eventually learn that life involves more than "a flick of the wrist" to acquire the good things they seek.

By word and example, you can help them use their God-given potential to give as well as to receive. This requires patience and perseverance but the results can have good effects for time and for eternity.

✦

"I will set My eyes upon them for good . . . I will build them up and not tear them down."
[JEREMIAH 24:6]

✦

Assist me, O Holy Spirit, to set a high standard for young people without being self-righteous.

What's in a Dandelion?

Mention dandelions and some people would be hard put to suggest even one use for them. But there are many.

For example, you can eat the roots, boiled and buttered; munch on the crowns, either cooked or as a salad; or chew on the blossoms properly prepared and seasoned.

Then you can wash the meal down with a glass of dandelion wine and finish things off with a steaming cup of "coffee" made from the versatile plant.

Most people would probably prefer to admire the uses of the dandelion than to try them out.

Nevertheless, the great diversity of such an ordinary commodity gives some hint of the potential that waits to be tapped in nature.

Even more, within each person created in God's image there are powers that can scarcely be imagined.

Stretch your powers of mind, heart and soul so that you will develop into the positive force for good that the Lord intended you to be.

✧

"The kingdom of heaven is like treasure hidden in a field." [MATTHEW 13:44]

✧

Never let me underestimate my abilities, O Lord, and help me put them to work for others.

Archeology in the Sky

Archeologists of the future may go up into the sky to un-cover some of the more interesting artifacts of our present civilization.

This is so because, since 1958, mankind has hurled more than 3,000 artificial objects into orbit.

For example, America's Vanguard satellite, weighing three pounds, was launched in 1958 and is not expected to come down till the year 2901.

Canada's Alluette I, sent aloft in 1962, won't fall out of orbit until 3796.

Dozens of other satellites are expected to continue whirl-ing in space until about the year 12,000.

The staggering vastness of time and space may at times compel any of us to think of ourselves as insignificant. How-ever, it is simply not true.

Everything we do, and even think, has real meaning in God's sight. He will work through us to effect far-reaching good, if only we let Him. We can accomplish things for others that passing centuries will never erase.

✧

"He who believes in Me will also do the works that I do; and greater works than these will he do." [JOHN 14:12]

✧

Enable us to grow in trust of Your providence, Father, and in the conviction that You are at work within us.

Get the Facts

When H. G. Wells noticed an unusually large stuffed bird in the drawing room of fellow writer, Henry James, he was perplexed and intrigued.

"My dear James," he asked, "what is that?"

"That," James informed him, "is a stork."

"Humph," Wells snorted, "it's not my idea of a stork."

"Apparently, however," James remarked, "it was God's idea of one."

It is a human tendency to assume that because one thinks something is right, it must be correct.

Conclusions drawn from sketchy information, rather than from complete facts, often lead to faulty and even dangerous reasoning.

In everything you think, say and do, make sure you get all the facts. Base your judgments on reality, not imagination.

Be particularly careful, too, to check whether your idea on any subject is fully in accord with "God's idea."

It will not only help in all your human relationships, but also keep you ever in tune with divine truth.

✧

"To get wisdom is better than gold; to get understanding is to be chosen rather than silver."
[PROVERBS 16:16]

✧

Give me the wisdom, O Holy Spirit, to distinguish between fact and fancy.

Washing Dishes Too Much for Him

A boy's aversion to washing dishes caused a lot of people considerable trouble not long ago in Michigan.

When the 12-year-old youngster was reported missing from his home, police organized a search party of 25 volunteers who spent most of the night combing the woods for him.

To everyone's surprise, the boy returned home under his own steam at 5 A.M., after dodging the searchers for 7 hours. When asked why he had run away, he replied: "It was my turn to wash the dishes."

People often spend more time and effort trying to dodge work than they would by cheerfully facing up to their responsibilities.

Show willingness and perseverance in fulfilling your share of obligations, both in and out of the home, and you will find your tasks will become more a joy than a drudgery.

God blesses those who eagerly and generously tackle their rightful tasks instead of running away from them.

✧

"By this My Father is glorified, that you bear much fruit." [JOHN 15:8]

✧

Let me gladly fulfill my duties, O Master, not try to evade them.

Helpful Hints for Speakers

Among the do's and don't's that experts recommend to inexperienced public speakers, the following deserve special consideration:

1. Do have something to say before you speak.
2. Don't apologize for your speech. If an excuse is necessary the talk shouldn't be given.
3. Do learn the art of brevity.
4. Don't tell your audience that you won't make a long speech and then proceed to do just that.
5. Don't repeat too much. Say what you have to say—make your point and then move on.
6. Do stop within the time limit given you.
7. Don't encroach upon the time of other speakers. Put yourself in their position.
8. Do adapt yourself to your audience rather than expect them to accommodate themselves to you.

God entrusts you with the power of speech. Whether you use it at home or at an outside meeting, give your listeners something worthwhile and at the same time show respect for their rights and feelings.

✧

"Death and life are in the power of the tongue." [PROVERBS 18:21]

✧

Thanks to You, O blessed Creator, for the privileges of being Your instrument in both word and deed.

Diversion in the Dentist's Chair

Going to the dentist is lots of fun for young patients of one doctor in Edmonton, Alberta.

Models of fish, horses and Royal Mounties hang from the office walls of the dentist who believes in putting his youthful patients in a playful mood. He also wears an assortment of brightly colored jackets.

The imaginative dentist covers his hypodermic needle with "magic cotton," which leads some children to remark that it "sure doesn't hurt with the cotton on it."

After the "tooth has gone to sleep," an instrument called a "Busy Bee" washes it out and another named "Woody Woodpecker" makes the filling.

Inconvenience, pain and trouble can sometimes be made more tolerable by distractions of one sort or another. In most cases, they are merely lessened, rather than avoided.

Serious hardships are best accepted and overcome by those who set out to be of some definite service to God and their fellow man. This is a point we could all check ourselves on.

✧

"If you faint in the day of adversity, your strength is small."   [PROVERBS 24:10]

✧

Bring me to a sense of maturity, O Jesus, by which I can face trouble courageously for Your sake.

Becomes Artist Through Teacher's Inspiration

A man who waited 40 years to become an artist will fulfill his dream when he retires this year.

"I have decided to dedicate the rest of my life completely to art," the U.N. employee said, recalling the comment of a childhood teacher that had inspired him: "You have God-given talent. Don't neglect it."

Lack of money and time forced the artistic Hollander to turn to other work. But always he continued to paint in all his spare time, exhibiting his work throughout New York State and winning honorable mention in the Prix de Paris competitions.

"I try to put a little bit of light, a little bit of a dream, and some truth into my work," the artist said. "I would try to quit, but then always the words of the teacher haunted me. I had to go back."

The power of a good teacher is hard to exaggerate. His is the unique privilege of working closely with parents to assist young people in bringing to maturity the great potential God has given them to make a solid contribution to life.

❖

"The Lord will guide you continually, and satisfy your desire with good things."

[ISAIAH 58: 11]

❖

Grant me the wisdom, O Holy Spirit, to help others use their gifts well.

Facts about Your Wonderful Feet

How far does the average American walk in his lifetime?

According to the magazine, *Today's Health*, most people walk about 65,000 miles, which is almost the same as trekking from New York to California and back again 13 times ... and all on the same pair of feet!

The article also points out that our feet are remarkable structural masterpieces. Each one, for example, contains no less than 26 bones, linked through 33 joints, secured together by 107 ligaments and supported by 19 muscles.

The intricacy of the human body from head to toe is cause for more than a little wonder.

Wonder should lead to gratitude to the divine Source of all we have and all we are.

Show effective thanks for your marvelous powers of body and soul by seeing to it that you spread respect for these gifts to everyone you meet.

However different men may be, in essentials we are all alike.

✣

"We will walk in the name of the Lord our God for ever and ever." [MICAH 4:5]

✣

Lead me step by step, O heavenly Father, to my eternal goal by applying Your love to every facet of life.

Too Many Dogs for the Catcher

Two days on the job convinced one dogcatcher that he had better find another niche in life.

The Philadelphia man resigned his position because, as he put it, "the township and the dogs are too big."

"There's no fooling the dogs," he conceded. "They let you chase them all over but by the time you get the net out —they're gone!"

Anyone who holds a position in the public interest, however large or small, deserves the thoughtful consideration of the people he serves.

By the same token, if you aspire to such a position yourself, be prepared for hardships, setbacks and suffering.

In times of discouragement when temptation comes to quit a difficult job, ask yourself what would happen if everybody decided to abdicate their responsibilities.

The Lord will bless you if you at least try to carry out the work you have undertaken. Once you have done your best, you can leave the rest to Him.

✢

"No one who puts his hand to the plow and looks back is fit for the kingdom of God."
[LUKE 9:62]

✢

Inspire me, O Lord, to keep problems in their proper perspective and high goals in sight.

Obedient Child Saves Mother's Life

A 5-year-old girl saved her mother's life because she did just what her mother told her to do.

The two were playing in the back yard of their home in Los Altos, Calif., when the ground collapsed under the mother, and plunged her into a septic tank.

Unable to get out, she told her daughter Nell to bring her the garden hose, which was attached to a faucet. Nell did and the mother wrapped it around her own neck to keep herself afloat.

Then, the mother instructed the child how to go to the telephone, dial "O" and ask for help. The operator connected the little girl with town officials. When asked where she lived, Nell replied unhesitatingly, "589 el Monte Avenue."

Firemen came immediately and rescued the mother.

In God's plan, there is no substitute for the thorough, fundamental training that a child should receive from its father and mother. The results can have effects for good throughout a lifetime.

✧

"Children, obey your parents in the Lord, for this is right." [EPHESIANS 6:1]

✧

Inspire parents, Holy Spirit, to imbue their children with wisdom and courage.

Laziness Is Costly

A young man who lost nearly 200 jobs for being late was recently arrested in London on the charge of stealing $56 from a friend.

When the judge told him to get out of bed and get busy, the lazy prisoner admitted: "I suppose I'm a day dreamer. I like lying in bed wishing I had a job with lots of money."

The old saying that "laziness is premature death" certainly applies to persons who try to idle their way through life. They not only fail to develop their capabilities but also stifle the very initiative that might lift them out of the doldrums.

You owe it to others as well as yourself to welcome, not evade, honest toil. Failure to shoulder your share of responsibilities means that others suffer in one way or another from your neglect.

Seek to find imaginative, constructive outlets for the powers of body, mind and soul that the Creator has entrusted to you. Then you will add special meaning to every job that you tackle.

✧

"Come to Me, all who labor and are heavy laden, and I will give you rest."

[MATTHEW 11:28]

✧

Grant, O Holy Spirit, that I may be diligent in fulfilling my responsibilities.

Polio Victim Rescues Drowning Tot

A woman crippled with polio unstrapped her steel leg braces and rescued a drowning 3-year-old boy after finding him floating face down in a 6-foot-deep water tank.

"I had to do something pretty quick," the 35-year-old woman explained later, "But I don't think I would have been able to help at all if I hadn't taken my leg irons off." Although she feared she would not be able to swim, she managed to reach the unconscious boy and pull him to the side.

For 10 minutes she applied artificial respiration, without success. She then tried mouth-to-mouth resuscitation until the boy finally stirred.

You would probably be amazed to discover what an enormous amount of untapped power and resourcefulness lies hidden within you. A generous Creator has put it in your keeping. But He doesn't want you to keep it to yourself.

Be on the lookout for the countless ways in which you can use this bit of divine greatness to help others in distress.

✧

"Bear one another's burdens, and so fulfill the law of Christ." [GALATIANS 6:2]

✧

Thanks, O Lord of Lords, for allowing me to be Your instrument in lightening the burdens of others.

Joys of Reading Denied to Millions

A Brazilian woman who had learned the rudiments of reading and writing in 40 hours of group instruction wrote this letter to the country's President:

"I beg you, sir, for scholarships for my children, because I can't educate them. I work day and night washing and ironing, so they shall not want. Their father, with six children, gets 50 cents for a day's service. How are we to get by?"

More than 700,000,000 people—one half of the world's adult population—are illiterate. The inability of adults to read and write hampers the educational progress of their children. In the home environment they often forget what they have learned in the classroom.

The job of providing the world's growing population with adequate opportunities for education, jobs, food and housing staggers the imagination. But few works are closer to the heart of Christ.

Even if you can't do much personally about world illiteracy, you may be able to encourage someone else who can.

✧

"*Encourage one another and build one another up.*" [1 THESSALONIANS 5:11]

✧

Help me, O Lord, to be tireless in seeking ways to share my own benefits with others less fortunate.

Boys Imitate Policeman Dads

Two small boys, both policemen's sons, captured a thief in a determined chase through a Brooklyn street.

The youngsters, 7 and 9, spotted a purse snatcher as he seized a woman's pocketbook. Going after him, they shouted: "You stole that lady's purse."

The thief ducked into a basement of a nearby apartment house, dropping the purse as he went. Retrieving it, the boys trailed the culprit to the basement.

To block the thief's escape, the boys pushed a plank and a washing machine against the door, and one ran out to call police. Officers arrived to arrest the trapped man a few minutes later.

Sons tend to imitate their fathers, both for better and for worse.

One man remarked that he was "awestruck by the power and influence that a father wields over his children in guiding their thoughts, hewing their future, shaping their way."

Parents who carry out their trust faithfully will receive a great reward from the Lord.

✧

"I urge you, then, be imitators of me."
[1 CORINTHIANS 4:16]

✧

Lord God, give fathers and mothers the firmness and gentleness they so much need.

AUGUST 16

Devotion Scores Over IQ

Contrary to popular opinion, IQ tests do not determine intelligence as a fixed, unchanging thing.

It would be more accurate to say that they measure the "learned responses" of an individual to a series of questions and problems.

Such tests are helpful to teachers in predicting the ability of youngsters to do academic work, but some students seem to elude any accurate measurement.

"A child may score in the 140's (a 'genius' rating) and yet be too lazy to read a book or do any of the tough groundwork and he'll fail at school," said John Stalnaker of the National Merit Scholarship Foundation.

"Another," he added, "may score much lower but by sheer devotion to his work, he'll succeed."

Whatever talents you have, whether few or many, they come to you from God. In return, He counts on you to live up to your potential by helping to build a world that will give Him glory by serving the best interests of all.

✧

"What have you that you did not receive?"
[1 CORINTHIANS 4:7]

✧

Let me show thanks each day, O heavenly Father, for all that You unfailingly give me.

One-Man Housing Clinic

A Puerto Rican businessman who refused to leave behind the problems of his neighbors received a $1,000 Lane Bryant Award for his work among minorities.

The 43-year-old claims adjuster for a New York law firm, a high-school dropout himself, has worked for 19 years as a one-man housing clinic for his neighbors in New York's Lower East Side.

He said that he could have gone to the suburbs when he escaped poverty himself, but he did not.

"When a person becomes involved in the attempt to bring about a change for the better," he explained, "that to me is success."

One way to find out the kind of people we are is to ask ourselves what success means to us.

If we can honestly say it is more than security, a fat pay check and personal gratification, there is reason for hope.

The Lord doesn't necessarily call us to extreme sacrifices for our neighbor. But He may be waiting for us to get beyond our present level of achievement.

✧

"Those who perform deeds of charity and of righteousness will have fullness of life."
[TOBIT 12:9]

✧

Spur me to a candid examination of conscience, Lord, and a resolve to follow Your will.

239

Glass of Water Brings Big Reward

A hospital attendant was astonished to learn that she had been left $280 in a will by a woman for whom she had performed but a single kindness.

The terms of the will made by a former hospital patient in Leicester, England, read simply:

"To Miss Jane Chapman, for her kindness in providing me with a glass of water when I requested it."

In the Gospels time and again the Lord reminds His hearers that attention to the physical as well as spiritual needs of others will be weighed in the judgment.

A glass of cold water, a word of heartfelt encouragement, a kindness done at personal sacrifice may never bring you an earthly reward. You may not even hear a word of thanks.

But such actions, done for love of God and neighbor, will someday bring to you the inspiring words:

❖

"Come, O blessed of My Father . . . for I was hungry and you gave me food, I was thirsty and you gave me drink." [MATTHEW 25:34]

❖

Move me, O Holy Spirit, to be generous and unmindful of self in coming to the aid of others.

Youngster Upsets Act

A strongman was embarrassed by a little girl while he was doing his act in the lobby of a theater in England where he doubles as a doorman.

"My daddy's stronger than you," the youngster chirped pleasantly.

The amused strongman picked up an iron bar and gently wrapped it around the neck of the 10-year-old. The only trouble was—he couldn't unwrap the rugged bar.

After several husky spectators tried and failed, firemen had to saw through the bar.

"I still think my daddy is stronger," was the little girl's reaction.

Her father, a former wrestler, conceded that he didn't do that sort of thing any more. Then he added: "But I'm proud of her for thinking of me as a strong man."

Children all over the world tend to admire and imitate their parents. This is as it should be, since fathers and mothers are placed there by God to guide and lead. Do whatever you can as a parent or counsellor to give young people something worth imitating.

❖

"Honor your father and your mother, as the Lord your God commanded you."
                                    [DEUTERONOMY 5:16]

❖

Make me always, O Lord, a source of inspiration for young people.

The Fisherman's Motto: Try Again

A battle between a huge sea bass and a young fisherman drew thousands of spectators to Cocoa Beach, Fla.

Bulletins over a local radio station aroused the interest of residents for miles around as the 15-year-old youth tried to land the sea bass.

After a 32-hour struggle, the boy's line snapped and the big fish swam free.

Undismayed by his lack of success, the plucky teenager told sympathetic friends: "Never mind, tomorrow we'll try again."

Even those who have never tried their luck with a fishing pole have to admire the determination of fishermen, whether their efforts are for sport or to make a living.

Perseverance and skill are two assets that eventually yield results, especially when the goal is a big one.

Even when such attempts end in failure, the Lord blesses those who sincerely try their best to improve the spiritual and material lot of others.

Remember these words: "Tomorrow we'll try again."

✧

"Do your best to present yourself to God as one approved, a workman who has no need to be ashamed." [2 TIMOTHY 2:15]

✧

Guard me against discouragement, O Lord, which would prevent me from being a good instrument in doing Your will.

Prisoner Changes His Mind

A prisoner who was sentenced to sit on a judge's bench for 10 days changed his attitude towards police and the administration of justice.

The 24-year-old factory worker had been found guilty of taunting a policeman in Indianapolis and saying "the police department is full of crooks."

The judge who heard the case felt that the young man should find out for himself that his opinion was neither true nor fair. So instead of imposing a fine or jail sentence, he ordered the man to sit beside him in municipal court for the next 10 days.

At the end of the period, the man wrote a memorandum. He said he was impressed with the careful weighing of all evidence and now believes in the honesty of the police and the integrity of the courts.

Much harm can be prevented if you make it a matter of conscience to get all the facts before making a final judgment about a person or group of people.

God expects each of us to be honest in all that we think, say and do.

✧

"Do not find fault before you investigate; first consider, and then reprove."
[SIRACH 11:7]

✧

Grant, O Lord, that I may treat others as fairly as I think they should treat me.

243

Computer Proves to Be Lifesaver

A cabin boy, seriously injured during a stormy Atlantic cross-ing, owes his life to the quick work of an electronic computer.

Since there was no doctor aboard the storm-tossed freighter, a distress signal was radioed to Coast Guard Headquarters in New York.

The officer on duty realized the Coast Guard could not reach the ship 2,000 miles away. So he called AMVER (Atlantic Merchant Vessel Report) headquarters, where the ship's position was fed into a computer.

The electronic machine instantly calculated the exact posi-tions of over 800 ships at sea and typed a list of those in the area with a doctor aboard.

A rendezvous was arranged with a French liner and the stricken boy was transferred into a surgeon's care only 62 minutes after the first call went out.

The marvels of modern technology, properly used, are a re-flection of God's Providence working through human means. Pray and work that they may always be used for man's libera-tion, never his enslavement.

✧

"The spirit of God has made me, and the breath of the Almighty gives me life."

[JOB 33:4]

✧

Grant, O Lord, that I may guide at least one competent person into a scientific career.

Self-Renewal Is a "Must"

A journalist from Wisconsin underlined the fact that leadership starts and re-starts in the hearts of each person. He wrote us at Christopher headquarters:

"I am a newspaper reporter. So often it is easy to lose sight of the real meaning of life, plodding along with the everyday stories of people's problems and injustices and, less frequently, their successes."

Then he added: "We all need insight into the role which we all are capable of filling by adding charity and the human aspect to our hurried lives."

A capacity for self-renewal is a "must" for anyone who wants to keep things in perspective and find continuing motivation for the accomplishment of the goals in life that really matter.

Re-examine from time to time the almost limitless possibilities for good that are open to you in the world.

Then look into yourself for the leadership resources of mind, heart and soul that the Lord will surely grant you to carry out your mission.

✧

"Be renewed in the spirit of your minds."
[EPHESIANS 4:23]

✧

Grant me the resiliency, O Holy Spirit, to get up again after each setback.

Science Demands Hard Work

The link between science and hard work was emphasized by Dr. Glenn T. Seaborg, Chairman of the U.S. Atomic Energy Commission. Here are some excerpts:

1. "Hard work," he said, "can be the most exciting kind of experience if it absorbs your interests so completely that you almost forget when mealtime comes."
2. Then he stressed the importance of motivation: "Or it can be boring and distasteful if the chore is one which you would never have undertaken voluntarily."
3. "The need for hard work as a basis for achievement is no less now than it ever was and only the rarest genius will reach the highest goals in science without expending his utmost effort."
4. "Not even the most wonderful environment will produce a scientist from a man or woman who is fundamentally allergic to hard work."

Whatever your job in life may be, you will be more certain to do it well if your efforts are grounded on trust in Christ, a desire to serve others—and hard work.

✧

"Whatever your task, work heartily, as serving the Lord." [COLOSSIANS 3:23]

✧

Let me labor perseveringly, O Lord, for the goals You want me to attain.

Fasts for Year, Loses 294 Pounds

A Scotsman recently ate his first meal in over a year. Breaking a total fast that reduced his weight from 473 pounds to a trim 179, the 26-year-old resident of Dundee, Scotland, ate one boiled egg, a slice of buttered bread and a cup of black coffee.

In a demonstration of will power that amazed doctors, the overweight man stopped eating for 392 days. During the entire period he lived only on plain water, soda water, tea and coffee, supplemented by special vitamin pills.

One doctor commented: "This is one of the most remarkable cases of voluntary weight reduction I ever heard of."

When a person of his own free will makes up his mind to be master of himself under the most trying circumstances, he often tames tendencies that no amount of outside pressure could force him to do.

God gives a special grace to you if you voluntarily do your part to bring out the best that is in you and conquer your weaknesses.

✦

"Each one must do as he has made up his mind, not reluctantly or under compulsion, for God loves a cheerful giver."
[2 CORINTHIANS 9:7]

✦

Lord, give me the will power I need to do good and avoid evil.

Woman Dies while 12 Look on

The cries of a drowning woman were ignored by a dozen people who stood by, watching, after her car plunged into the Great Miami River in Ohio.

A witness said the 50-year-old motorist, stranded on the roof of her car, kept screaming: "I can't swim." None of the 12 spectators responded.

As the car slowly sank she made a desperate attempt to save herself by jumping into the water. She "kicked around a little," the witness added, but then she disappeared.

The drowned woman's body was recovered and identified by police. She had apparently been on her way to work when her car skidded off the road and rolled down a 25-foot embankment into the river.

This woman's death dramatizes a frightening trend. More and more people are electing to observe disaster from a safe distance.

Dare to "become involved" when the physical or spiritual well-being of another is at stake. You will be a true Christbearer if you do.

✧

"But a Samaritan, as he journeyed, came to where he was; and when he saw him, he had compassion." [LUKE 10:33]

✧

In meeting the dangers of our times, O divine Master, teach me how to be daring without being reckless.

Teenager Pays Debts before Death

Before an 18-year-old boy died of leukemia in a Cartersville, Georgia, hospital, he had the satisfaction of knowing his debts were entirely paid.

During his protracted illness, the youth endeavored to meet his medical expenses by working with a highway construction crew. But he was able to earn only a small portion of what he owed.

The determination of the teenager to settle all his accounts despite his illness caused widespread admiration. News stories about him aroused so much sympathy that gifts and pledges totaling $1,400 were donated to his cause.

Shortly before his death, the boy's parents brought him the good news that all his bills had been "paid in full."

To make a conscientious effort to meet all of one's financial obligations is a credit to anyone. It can be also a forceful reminder of the importance of preparing as thoroughly for the final accounting at the Judgment Seat of God.

✧

"So each of us shall give account of himself to God."   [ROMANS 14:12]

✧

Teach me, O divine Master, to be faithful in fulfilling my debts, both temporal and spiritual.

Too Much for a Pup

A pup suffering from acute indigestion was taken to a veterinary in England. He discovered that the dog had swallowed the following items:

Two diamond rings, two lengths of leather harness, several lumps of coal and wood, a small magnet, three metal springs, a harness buckle, a metal carton lid and an inch-long nail.

Surveying the assortment, the veterinary exclaimed: "Easily a national record."

While animals are hardly responsible for what they do, any human being who thinks he can think, say, do or even eat anything he likes is inviting mental, spiritual or physical "indigestion."

God entrusts each of us with a free will. But with that divine gift goes a tremendous responsibility.

By upholding good and rejecting evil we prove to Him that we truly appreciate the great privilege of freedom of choice.

Be selective in your thoughts, words and deeds and you will be functioning as a complete human being.

✧

"Live sober, upright, and godly lives in this world."   [TITUS 2:12]

✧

Thanks to You, O generous Creator, for endowing me with the power to choose between right and wrong.

What Is a Wife Worth?

The average housewife puts in a 99-hour week and is worth $159 to her family, according to a survey conducted by the Chase Manhattan bank.

Furthermore, it estimated that the 30 million homemakers of the country, while performing an irreplaceable service, make a yearly contribution to the economy of nearly 250 million dollars.

The estimate was based on wages varying from $1.50 to $2.50 an hour in such duties as: nursemaid . . . dietitian . . . food buyer . . . cook . . . dishwasher . . . housekeeper . . . laundress . . . seamstress . . . practical nurse . . . maintenance man . . . gardener . . . and chauffeur.

Far more than any statistical chart can indicate, the millions of homemakers throughout the country and over the world constitute one of mankind's greatest hopes for peace and happiness.

Since God has ordained that the woman is the heart of the family, husbands and children should acknowledge this fact by appreciation, cooperation, and in particular by sincere love and affection.

✧

"Husbands, love your wives."

[EPHESIANS 5:25]

✧

Awaken me, O Jesus, to the irreplaceable value that homemakers contribute to the good of the world.

She Put Teeth into Her Warning

A well-timed bite by a 4-year-old girl with a good sense of smell saved her family from gas poisoning.

A peculiar odor awakened the child at 3 o'clock one morning and she hurried to her father's room to tell him.

When a vigorous shake failed to disturb his peaceful slumber, she bit him on the arm. That turned the trick.

The police discovered that the strange smell was caused by monoxide fumes from the family car which had been left running in the adjoining garage.

The parents and all 3 children were in good condition after being administered a dose of oxygen.

The inborn urge to preserve one's own life and that of loved ones reveals itself in many ways. Deepen and broaden this instinct in young people. You can help them develop a Christlike regard for their own family, and also for those who need their help in the community, nation and world.

✧

"A new commandment I give to you, that you love one another."   [JOHN 13:34]

✧

Inspire me with Your grace, O holy Father, to show gratitude for Your benefits by extending them to others.

Live Longer by Living More Fully

Older people who keep busy actually live longer, according to an experimental program conducted at 3 nursing homes in Vancouver, B.C.

The patients, all older persons, were divided into 2 groups. One was given normal nursing-home care, the other an "activation program." The latter group was urged to feed and dress themselves and to engage in activities such as handicrafts and hobbies instead of staying in bed.

A year after the program was started, 64 per cent of the active group were still alive, compared to the 45 per cent of the inactive group.

Moreover 18 per cent of the active patients had improved so much that they were discharged, whereas only 5 per cent of the inactive ones were able to return to their homes.

Live a more meaningful, happier life—and a longer one— by finding constructive outlets for your physical, intellectual and spiritual energies.

Put to good use the power that God has entrusted to you personally for as long as you have life and you will be happier both here and hereafter.

❖

"Teach us to number our days that we may get a heart of wisdom."   [PSALM 90:12]

❖

May I use well, O Lord, the time and talent You have loaned to me.

New Electric Safety Device for Cars

A laser beam that will keep cars at a safe distance from each other is one of the newest automotive devices.

The laser, "too gentle to take the fuzz off a fly's legs," operates in the front of a car. It either emits a warning noise or starts braking whenever it detects another car coming too close.

The low-power laser and seven other electronic devices were designed by General Electric Company to do jobs that driver and mechanical parts cannot do.

As the number of automobiles on our highways multiplies, safeguards for drivers and pedestrians are needed in greater numbers.

Motorists have a heightened responsibility to think before they act. Auto makers must keep designing vehicles for safety as well as beauty. And workers should be increasingly attentive to small details in assembly construction.

Every segment of society has a duty to God and other people to show responsibility for human life.

✧

"None of us lives to himself, and none of us dies to himself." [ROMANS 14:7]

✧

Alert me, Holy Spirit, to my responsibility to look out for the best interests of all people.

Bubbles Baffle Shark

Strange as it sounds, blowing bubbles is one way to scare off a marauding shark.

A soldier in Brisbane, Australia, tried this unusual procedure and found it worked fine. Here's his account of what happened when a shark approached as he and a friend were swimming 400 yards offshore:

"I took a deep breath and dived straight at it," he said. "I blew out air and made bubbles."

"Then I turned and swam as fast as possible for the shore. I do not know what happened to the shark."

Although it isn't every day that a shark will get within biting distance of most of us, the swimmer's action points out that courage involves: 1) quick thinking in the presence of danger; and 2) reasonable precaution in avoiding needless harm.

The towering problems of war and peace, of economic and social development, of human rights and personal responsibility all need your courageous and Christlike response if the world is to be made a better place.

✧

"Be strong and of good courage . . . He will not fail you or forsake you."

[DEUTERONOMY 31:6]

✧

Help me, O Lord, to take a stand, not only for my own rights but also for those of others.

Alert Laborer Saves Own Life

A hatful of air saved one worker from being buried alive.

The 39-year-old man was working at the bottom of a flood control trench in Los Angeles when fellow laborers shouted that one side of the ditch was collapsing.

Realizing that he couldn't get out of the way in time, the resourceful man clapped his metal hat over his mouth and waited for 15 minutes under a 4-foot pile of debris.

The tiny bit of air in his hat was just enough to keep the workman from suffocating. When his companions finally dug him out, he was shaken but unharmed. He was completely revived with a few whiffs of oxygen.

Quick thinking and alert action under the most discouraging circumstances can often turn seeming defeat into victory.

God has given you a greater reserve of imagination and daring than you probably realize. You can honor Him by bringing it into play in everyday life as well as in emergencies.

✧

"Be not frightened, neither be dismayed; for the Lord your God is with you wherever you go."   [JOSHUA 1:9]

✧

Thanks, O generous Master, for the many physical and spiritual blessings You have entrusted to me.

How Much Do You Care?

The word *"apathetic"* is often applied to people who take a "don't care" attitude about improving civic life, schools, labor-management relations or the state of current literature.

It is used, too, in regard to persons who don't lift a finger to rescue someone under attack or in an accident.

"Apathy" is derived from two Greek words: *"a"* meaning "away from," and *"pathos,"* signifying "suffering." At the root of all apathy, therefore, is the reluctance to suffer.

The dictionary describes it with such expressions as "indifference . . . lack of interest . . . insensibility . . . lethargy . . . unconcern . . . innate sluggishness . . . lack of feeling . . . stupor . . . hardness of heart."

One of the best ways to avoid apathy is to shake off a self-centeredness that is blind to the needs and rights of others. Then, as God's instrument, try to show them the same divine solicitude in trouble that you would want and expect if you were in their plight.

✧

"If a blind man leads a blind man, both fall into a pit." [MATTHEW 15:14]

✧

Let me be so anxious to help my fellow man, O Lord, that I will not have time to be apathetic.

She Solved the Mystery

Being very closely followed by a strange car was most disturbing for a woman driver in Globe, Arizona.

After three blocks, she could stand it no longer, and pulled over to the curb. But the car behind trailed right along and stopped at the curb too.

Determined to find out what was up, the woman driver jumped out to investigate.

To her surprise and horror, she discovered that she had been towing another automobile, whose bumper had caught in her own car in a parking lot.

Before jumping to conclusions, it is always wise to stop a moment and check the facts. You will prevent yourself from making an error in judgment that could be harmful to others or to yourself.

Much trouble is caused in these critical times because person after person fails to get the full truth before making a judgment that is both incomplete and unfair.

Be slow to judge and thorough in distinguishing between fact and fiction and you will be blessed by both God and man.

✧

"Do not judge by appearances, but judge with right judgment." [JOHN 7:24]

✧

Grant, O Holy Spirit, that I may never grow weary in the pursuit of truth.

Find Purpose in Your Work

Without so much as a blush, a meter reader in England admitted that he had never read a water meter in the last 7 years.

"Some were in pig-sties," he said, "others in haystacks. One was even in a field with a big bull. Many meant a dirty job of digging down to them. They were not like light and gas meters—easy to get at."

He explained that about 7 years before he gave up trying. From then on, he resorted to sheer guess work, relying on water bills from previous years.

"I liked everything about the job," he admitted, "except reading those meters. They became a bore."

Nobody likes "dirty jobs." But, like it or not, they have to be done.

Stop to think every so often about why God put you into this world. By directing your activities in the light of eternity, you will be more likely to be so busy helping other people that you won't have time to be bored. The stakes are so high in this nuclear age that none of us can afford to be mediocre.

✧

"*And every work that he undertook . . . seeking his God, he did with all his heart.*"
[2 CHRONICLES 31:20]

✧

Let me view each task, O Lord, as another opportunity to serve you and my fellow man.

SEPTEMBER 7

The Hidden Face of Crime

The quiet-looking individual who pockets a few dollars that are not his can cause a greater loss to society than the masked bank robber.

This is the opinion of James V. Bennett, who was head of the federal prison system for 28 years.

"White collar crime," he said, "composes the vast bulk of our crime problem. Its large mass lies iceberg-like below the lesser bulk of such visible crimes as auto-theft, bank robbery and burglary."

Mr. Bennett cited a study showing that only one out of ten bank embezzlements is reported to authorities.

Laws, police, courts and prisons can touch only a small portion of the problems related to crime.

It is up to millions of people like you: 1) to determine that their own actions are distinguished by integrity; 2) to assist law enforcement agencies when required; 3) to seek ways to eliminate conditions that breed certain forms of crime; and 4) to press for procedures that safeguard the God-given as well as constitutional rights of every citizen without exception.

✧

"Do you not know that the unrighteous will not inherit the kingdom of God?"
[1 CORINTHIANS 6:9]

✧

Let me encourage respect for just laws, O Jesus, by obeying them myself even when it hurts.

Win People, Don't Repel Them

"People are something like turtles," was one man's sage comment to his grandson.

The two had been out walking in the countryside when the youngster happened on a small land turtle. As he tried to examine his find, the turtle promptly retired into its shell. Just as promptly, the boy picked up a stick and tried to pry the shell open.

"That will never get you anywhere," remarked the older man. "Let me show you how." And with that he took the turtle into the house. After a few minutes on the warm hearth, the turtle stuck out its head and feet and started crawling towards the boy.

Then came the observation about people and turtles. "Never try to force a fellow into anything," was the old man's advice. "Just warm him up with a little kindness and he'll probably respond."

Brusque, harsh or tactless methods usually do more harm than good. Learn from Christ Himself. His gentle, loving approach is one we all should imitate.

✧

"Learn from Me; for I am gentle and lowly in heart." [MATTHEW 11:29]

✧

Help me, O Lord, to show the warmth and gentleness that are true signs of Your love.

Takes Financial Loss to Be a Teacher

Not many people would take a 50 per cent salary cut to go into college teaching. One 47-year-old executive did just that ... and has no complaints.

Besides a desire to find a change of pace from his hectic business pursuits, he gave this as his reason: "I believe very strongly in higher education and the importance of stimulating intellectual curiosity in young people."

The growing school population gives fresh emphasis to the importance of the need for talented and dedicated teachers on every level of the educational ladder.

Even though you may not be in a position to go into teaching yourself, you can: 1) encourage and try to cooperate with teachers; 2) point out to young people the great service to God and humanity they can render by a career in education.

You may achieve far-reaching effects for good if you do.

✧

"So we are ambassadors for Christ, God making His appeal through us."
[2 CORINTHIANS 5:20]

✧

Let me assist the cause of learning, O Lord, in every way I can.

Potato Chips Galore

A Scotsman claims the world's championship for eating potato chips.

The 20-year-old Glasgow contender won the title after downing 30 bags of salted chips. It took him just 56 minutes to consume nearly 5 lbs. of the crispy delicacy.

His feat displaced the previous claimant, a Northumberland miner, who had managed to swallow 29 bags in 62 minutes, 6 years ago.

Men will tax themselves to the extremes of endurance once they set their hearts on achieving any goal, be it good, bad or indifferent.

They demonstrate time and again that "where there is a will, there is a way."

God has entrusted to you a bit of His greatness. This divine power within you is waiting to be released. But make sure that it is channeled in the right direction, not dissipated on mere whims.

You will derive much satisfaction from life if you use your physical, mental and spiritual energy for the good of others, not only for your own pleasure.

✧

"Be wise as serpents and innocent as doves."
[MATTHEW 10:16]

✧

Inspire me, O Holy Spirit, to put my heart into the things that count.

Tragic World of Addiction

One narcotics addict described his tragic bout with marijuana and heroin in these grim words: "It's like the whole world had shut me out."

After he was hospitalized, the 31-year-old man told how he had almost died of an overdose, how he tried to hide his plight from his wife and how it had caused deep anguish to his mother.

"It's a dream world, you see, but you're never really happy," he explained.

The number of drug addicts in the U.S. runs into countless thousands. Estimates for New York City alone range from 21,000 to more than twice that figure.

But the ruined lives, family disruption, vice and crime can never be adequately measured.

Conditions such as extreme poverty, mental illness, overcrowding, and broken homes prepare the way for evils such as addiction.

Press for just laws that will help the addict to obtain essential treatment, and so perform a Christlike service to improve the spiritual and temporal welfare of mankind.

✧

"Let our people learn to apply themselves to good deeds, so as to help cases of urgent need."   [TITUS 3:14]

✧

Stimulate me, O Lord, to help—not just in word but in action—those who are in trouble.

264

32 Days on Smokestack

Perching on top of a 131-foot smokestack of the factory where he worked in Okinawa was one man's way of dramatizing work grievances.

But after 32 days atop the chimney, the 27-year-old striker ended his long vigil of protest.

Blackened by soot and grime, the disheartened worker described his prolonged stay on the smokestack as an agonizing one.

In trying to correct abuses, make sure you are on the side of justice. Ask yourself questions such as these:

1. Have I got all the facts, or am I acting on incomplete knowledge?
2. Am I truly interested in seeking solutions fair to all? Or, by taking a dramatic stand, am I more interested in drawing attention to myself?
3. Do I make a sincere effort to be constructive, or am I only a complainer and fault-finder?

Strive to be God's instrument by helping to settle differences rather than widen them.

✧

"Blessed are the peacemakers, for they shall be called children of God." [MATTHEW 5:9]

✧

Enlighten me, O Holy Spirit, so that I will think and act fairly, not emotionally.

Teacher's Regard for Class Pays Off

The first day of school began on a bright note for a teacher who was glancing over the class roll.

After each student's name was a number, such as 138, 140 and 145.

"Look at these IQ's," she thought to herself. "I've got a terrific class."

As a result, the elated teacher tried new methods. The students responded exceptionally well to her creative approach.

Only later did she find out that the figures after each pupil's name stood, not for IQ, but for their locker numbers.

It is often startling what can happen when those in positions of authority, such as parents or teachers, treat those in their charge in a positive way. If one must make a choice, misplaced confidence is preferable to defeatism.

We act in harmony with the Creator as often as we try to find the potential for achievement in others and build realistically on it.

✧

"Sanctify them in the truth; Your word is truth."   [JOHN 17:17]

✧

Enable us to get beyond feelings of hopelessness about people, Lord, as we strive to assist them.

Teenager Hooks Baby Carriage

One youngster made what may be the catch of his career while he was angling in a London park.

The 13-year-old was fishing when a stroller with a baby in it rolled down a sloping bank and sank into the pond, disappearing from view.

The quick-thinking boy pulled the carriage—baby and all —to safety with his fishing line.

Anyone who has saved even one life during his time on earth has reason to be grateful.

Occasionally we ought to set aside a few minutes to consider the value of the human person.

It has taken mankind thousands of years to arrive at the high esteem in which the human person is now held. Even yet, our theories far outrun our practice.

It is above all as a child of God, created in the image of his Father, that each human being should be regarded. Fortified by that vision, we are far more likely to make concerted efforts to protect and promote the dignity of all men in every way we can.

✧

"See what love the Father has given us, that we should be called children of God; and so we are."　　　　　　　　[1 JOHN 3:1]

✧

Help me see in each member of the human race, Father, a reflection, however dim, of Your image.

267

Share Your Benefits, Don't Hoard Them

A remarkable cure for asthma tragically vanished with the doctor who developed it. It could have been an untold boon to millions of sufferers.

A friend congratulated him for his discovery which was so effective that it worked in 8 out of 10 cases. "You ought to put it on the market so it can reach more people," he said.

But the good doctor was so preoccupied with his own patients that he never got around to making his findings available to the public at large.

Not long after the marketing possibilities were pointed out to him, he died—and his cure died with him.

Seldom does the failure of one person to "deliver" his advantage to others result in the loss of so much to so many. But God expects each of us—not only the highly talented— to make positive contributions to the good of all.

Rather than "hide your light under a bushel," seek ways to put your time and talents to work for everyone.

❖

"Give and it will be given to you."

[LUKE 6:38]

❖

Help me to be a distributor of Your blessings,
O Lord, and not to keep them to myself.

Finds Son Locked in Mail Box

Hearing cries from a mail box prompted a woman in Birmingham, England, to do a little investigating.

She could hardly believe her eyes when she discovered her own weeping 5-year-old son peering sadly through the letter slot of the locked compartment.

A hurried phone call was made to the local post office and a postman soon arrived to let the little boy out of the mail box.

Upon questioning, he admitted that while playing, he had pulled on the door of the mail box, found it open, and then climbed inside. He had planned to get out in a few minutes, but meanwhile his 8-year-old cousin slammed the door on him.

Curiosity that is not based on prudence causes woe for young and old alike. But excessive fear of getting into trouble should not lead to the other extreme of avoiding everything that involves resourcefulness.

Make it your business to bring out the power for good which God has entrusted to you by being imaginative, generous and reasonably careful.

✧

"Set up waymarks for yourself, make yourself guideposts, consider well the highway."
[JEREMIAH 31:21]

✧

Teach me, O Lord, to be daring without being reckless.

Round the World in a Small Boat

A 65-year-old Englishman, Sir Francis Chichester, who had sailed the Atlantic six times now has circumnavigated the globe alone!

He covered the 28,500 miles in 226 days in a 53-foot ketch. First he sailed 13,750 miles from England via Australia around the Cape of Good Hope, Africa's tip.

The enterprising sailor then completed his round-the-world trip by sailing around Cape Horn, the tip of South America, and back to Plymouth, England. There have been only eight attempts to sail around Cape Horn in a small boat, and six ended in disaster.

Asked why he was making the long and dangerous sail, the adventurer replied: "Because I've got a great passion to make it. That's the basic reason."

A person driven by an intense desire to achieve a definite objective invariably accomplishes far more than an individual without aim or purpose.

In working for God, self and others, set big and worthy goals for yourself and you will add much breadth and meaning to your life.

✧

"When you pass through the waters I will be with you." [ISAIAH 43:2]

✧

Imbue me with bigness of vision, Holy Spirit, so that I may lead a more productive life.

Judge Favors Parrot

Polly can ask for a cracker any time and in any way she pleases, according to one magistrate's ruling.

The parrot's owner was brought into an Ohio court on a charge that his pet was disturbing the peace by whistling, screaming and hollering day and night.

But Polly was saved on a technicality. The judge threw out the case on the grounds that the law specifies that a disturbance of the peace may be caused only by the use of horns, bells, radios or other instruments or devices.

While there may be legitimate differences of opinion as to how much it takes to disturb the peace, all of us have a built-in standard of what is approximately reasonable.

It is concisely summed up in the divine rule stressed by Christ when He said: "As you wish that men would do to you, do so to them."   [LUKE 6:36]

By showing others the same consideration that you would expect if you were in their circumstances, you will be sure to strike a happy balance in respecting their rights as well as protecting your own.

✧

Help me to look at things from the other person's point of view, O Lord.

He Just Couldn't Sit Still

One industrious man left the bus station where he was waiting in a better condition than he found it.

He complained he was "going crazy" doing nothing. So he pulled a brush out of his luggage and offered to give the small place a quick coat of paint.

The pleased manager bought paint for the hard-working traveler and 2 hours later the interior of the station had a bright new coat.

Then he hopped aboard his bus.

Now and then we meet the rare individual who must be "up and doing" at all times. Such a trait can be carried to excess, but most of us are more likely to slide off in the other direction. The proper use of the relatively short stay we are given on earth is a never-ending challenge.

The Lord wants us to set aside adequate periods for rest and recreation. But He also wants us to employ our few years on earth in developing good work habits and applying our talents to the service of others.

✧

"Those who plan good have joy."
[PROVERBS 12:20]

✧

Instill in me, O Lord, the discipline needed to get the most out of life by putting the most into it.

The Missing Shopping Carts

It's no small headache for supermarkets to keep customers from disappearing with the shopping carts provided for their convenience.

As things stand, about 500,000 of these carts disappear from the premises each year, never to return.

At a cost of $30 a cart, this amounts to a loss of $15 million annually, plus the further expense of trying to retrieve the missing carts.

Shoppers often push the carts out of stores into the parking lots pretending to unload purchases into a car. But, instead, they just push them on home.

Most of the carts are eventually abandoned. For example, 108 of them recently turned up in a dredging operation in a river near Boston.

Still again, some are converted into laundry carts, portable shoeshine stands and barbecue grills.

This is just one more reminder that an honest world starts with each of us. Check on yourself to make sure that in thought, word and deed you act with the realization that you are always in God's presence.

✧

"The eyes of the Lord are in every place,
keeping watch on the evil and the good."
[PROVERBS 15:3]

✧

Help me, O Holy Spirit, to be as honest towards others as I wish them to be to me.

Sits Up in Coffin

Weeping relatives got the jolt of their lives while they knelt and prayed around a coffin in Ostrov, Rumania. The occupant surprised them by suddenly sitting up, very much alive.

The supposedly dead man, a farmer, had received a severe shock from contact with a power line and had appeared to die. In fact, a death certificate had been issued.

However, 12 hours later, the man came out of his stupor. Upon awakening he was understandably surprised to find himself in a coffin, ready for burial. Fortunately, the lid had not yet been sealed, so he was able to open it and rejoin his relatives.

The chances are remote indeed that any of us will be involved in such an unlikely mistake. But sooner or later each of us will be summoned by the angel of death to render an account of our stewardship.

Pause and reflect prayerfully from time to time on the profound questions: Who am I? Where do I come from? Where am I going? How do I get there?

✧

"We shall all stand before the judgment seat of God." [ROMANS 14:10]

✧

Teach me so to live, O Lord, that I will always be prepared to die.

Back to School in Life's Twilight

These are the words of a 104-year-old woman: "If I die to-morrow, I want to be able to write my name."

That was the reason a frail grandmother gave to teachers when she registered for adult education classes at a junior college in Texas.

The white-haired little woman said that her parents had been poor. The long hours she worked as a child left no time for school. Mentally and physically agile despite her years, she has already mastered the fundamentals of reading and writing.

"There's one thing I'm not going to let anybody do," she says, "and that's to let them stop me from getting my education."

It is always heartening to learn of people who keep trying to expand their horizons right to the end of the days God has allotted to them.

Whether you are 14, 64 or 104, never stop in your efforts to gain knowledge so that you may share your talents with the world.

❖

"Wisdom is better than jewels, and all that you may desire cannot compare with her."
[PROVERBS 8:11]

❖

Keep me young in spirit, Lord, so that I may remain open to new possibilities.

Toddler Shows Remarkable Aim

His sleeping father's open mouth was too much of a temptation for a year-old toddler in England.

With remarkable accuracy, he popped a half-crown (about 35¢ and the size of a half-dollar) into the 29-year-old truck driver's mouth.

The man swallowed the coin and woke up with a start. When he realized what had happened, he rushed to the hospital.

After removal of the object, he commented that one thing his son didn't have was a toy bank. Then he added: "But it will be the first thing I buy him when I get home."

Jumping at opportunities is something that young people can be counted on to do, from teenagers down to the youngest. Often the results are refreshing—sometimes they are disconcerting.

Parents and those who are in contact with youth have many God-given opportunities to inspire them not only to help themselves but also to serve others. Use your own opportunities to best advantage.

✧

"So then, as we have opportunity, let us do good to all men." [GALATIANS 6:10]

✧

Grant me the vision, O Lord, to see the potential in the young, and the grace to bring it out to best effect.

Check on Yourself

A ship's chief engineer got a reply he scarcely expected from a fireman recently assigned to his crew.

He saw the young man for the first time on a routine visit to the engine room. "How long have you been working down here?" he asked.

"Ever since I saw you coming down the ladder," was the new arrival's frank answer.

Those who fulfill their responsibilities only when someone is checking up on them seldom make much of their lives. They shortchange others by failing to live up to their obligations, but they cheat themselves even more.

Wherever you are, or whatever you do, you are always in the presence of God. And you are ultimately responsible to Him for all that you think, say and do.

If you are constantly motivated by this inspiring thought, you will find an increasing joy and satisfaction in life. And you will conscientiously perform your duties at home, on the job and everywhere else, whether anyone is watching you or not.

✧

"Behold, now is the acceptable time; behold, now is the day of salvation!"
[2 CORINTHIANS 6:2]

✧

It is a consolation, O Lord, to know that You know my every thought, word and deed.

Saves Friend under Subway Train

Would you jump into the path of an onrushing subway train to save the life of a friend?

One heroic young woman, 28, did that when her friend, 26, fainted and fell off the platform and onto the tracks in a New York subway station.

Onlookers feared the worst when they saw a train enter the station just as the courageous girl leaped. They saw her pull her unconscious friend into the trough between the tracks and then lie down beside her.

The oncoming train came to a screeching stop but not until 3 cars had passed over them. When workmen found the two friends, neither was seriously hurt.

Times of crisis often reveal the greatness of love hidden within our hearts and the lengths to which we will go to sacrifice ourselves in behalf of others.

Try to display this same Christlike solicitude for others in the humdrum of daily life, as well as in emergencies. You are bound to leave the world better than you found it.

✧

"Greater love has no man than this, that a man lay down his life for his friends."

[JOHN 15:13]

✧

Teach me, O divine Savior, to show the same daring in helping others that I would wish for myself.

Music Tightens Family Bonds

One enjoyable way to span the communication gap in family life is to develop a shared interest in music.

No one seems to know how many families in the United States have two or more musicians, but the number is increasing, according to the American Music Conference. In all, a record 37 million individuals play musical instruments.

"Parents who play with their youngsters set good examples —not just of musicianship, but of honest enthusiasm," says a report of the AMC.

Parents who share a musical interest with their children find that it is not only worth it—but that it can be real fun.

By strengthening the bonds of family life, fathers and mothers build bridges of communication and pathways to the future.

God's blessing rests upon those who help others to a deeper appreciation of the wonders of His creation and who develop their latent abilities.

✧

"Behold, my servants shall sing for gladness of heart."   [ISAIAH 65:14]

✧

Enable me to grow in understanding of music, Lord, even if I do not play an instrument myself.

Cancer-Stricken Doctor Bids Farewell

A doctor critically ill with cancer inserted this notice in a New England weekly newspaper:

"I regret to announce that due to illness that will perhaps be a prolonged one, I will no longer be able to serve you as your family physician.

"I wish to take this opportunity to thank my many loyal and faithful patients and friends for the good will they have shown me for the past 35 years.

"May God be with you."

The doctor's wife explained that he was anxious to let people know he was no longer at his office, to save them the trouble and disappointment of going only to find he was not practicing.

The quick and generous devotion of the afflicted physician to young and old alike for 35 years had won him the friendly accolade of the "fastest doctor in town."

Kindness never becomes old-fashioned. Show a Christlike concern for every person you can reach in life and you will begin your heaven on earth.

❖

"Behold, how good and pleasant it is when brothers dwell in unity!" [PSALM 133:1]

❖

Let me be a co-worker with You, O divine Master, in bringing Your love to all men.

He Missed His Friends in Jail

An ex-prisoner became so homesick for his old friends behind bars that he decided to commit some offense that would enable him to serve another term in the Georgia State Prison.

In an attempt to get quick action, the 67-year-old man tossed a rock through a post office window. But he soon found out that this only defeated his purpose.

Since damaging a post office is a federal offense, he faced the prospect of ending up in a federal prison—where he didn't have any friends at all.

Giving in to the temptation to use unworthy means to achieve any objective usually worsens an already bad situation.

Rather than compound mistakes, strive to rise above any and all inducements to compromise. Our Lord will give you every help you need, if you patiently and generously try to uphold what is right and just.

Then, too, the more you develop your own sense of integrity, the better able you will be to strengthen those who may not have the courage of their convictions.

✧

"Cast off the works of darkness and put on the armor of light." [ROMANS 13:12]

✧

Keep me mindful, O Jesus, that I should always uphold truth, not trifle with it.

Book Returned after 40 Years

It took over 40 years for one reader to return his book to a public library.

He was due to bring it back on July 22, 1922 but despite whatever good intentions he had, he kept putting it off. With each passing week, month and year, the fines mounted.

Finally in January 1963, the library announced that overdue books could be returned without the usual penalty.

This forgiving attitude struck a responsive chord in the negligent "book borrower" and the long-missing volume found its way back to the library shelves.

A library official said that had the fine been imposed, it would have amounted to $124.23. Then he wryly added: "Maybe he was a slow reader."

Reasonable forgiveness opens many a door that might otherwise remain shut. It brings into play that quality of mercy that all of us hope for when we make mistakes.

As Alexander Pope said: "To err is human, to forgive divine."

✧

"If you do not forgive men their trespasses, neither will your Father forgive your trespasses." [MATTHEW 6:15]

✧

Let me show others in trouble, O Jesus, the same understanding that I expect for myself.

Boy Dies Trying to Reach Mother

A lonely 9-year-old boy died trying to walk 30 miles home to his mother one winter day.

The homesick youngster had been boarding for the previous 4 months at a boys' ranch in Goldsmith, Texas. He set out on foot one night on the long hike to his home.

When he had gone 5 miles, a truck driver offered him a lift. But his mother had told him not to ride with strangers. So he said no.

By sundown the next day he had made 15 miles—halfway home. Suddenly a howling wind from the north dropped the temperature to 11 degrees. It was too much for the boy. His frozen body was found in a mesquite clump where he had sought shelter.

"He wanted to see his mother," a ranch employee said. "He was just 9 years old. Those kids don't have too much motherly love. They crave affection."

Children require many things. But above all else they need the love and understanding that God means to send them through parents and others.

"Be you, therefore, imitators of God, as very dear children and walk in love."

[EPHESIANS 5:1]

✧

May I serve as an instrument of Your love, O Lord.

The Protest Came Too Late

One woman became visibly upset when she saw a policeman in Berlin, N.H., writing out a parking ticket for her car.

"Officer," she protested, "this is my first ticket in more than 20 years."

As the patrolman handed the unwelcome piece of paper to the unhappy motorist, he sympathetically replied: "We'll both have something to remember. This is the first ticket I've ever given out."

No amount of pleading after the fact can wholly undo the harm caused by an unwise action. At best, it can serve as a warning for steering clear of future misconduct.

Far better to show a little foresight in anticipating difficulties that may confront us than spend valuable time "crying over spilt milk."

Use the common sense God gave you to weigh the consequences of your actions. You will be more effective not only in protecting your own best interests but also in safeguarding the rights of others.

✧

"A man is commended according to his good sense." [PROVERBS 12:8]

✧

Grant me the wisdom, O heavenly Father, to see ahead so that I may always act with discretion.

Kansas Girl Does Her Bit in Pakistan

Three bicycle accidents, a broken arm, a bout of hepatitis and a slight concussion were par for the course to a determined young woman from Kansas working with the Peace Corps in Pakistan. To top it all off, she has re-enlisted for another year.

When a 27-year-old nurse arrived in Peshawar, West Pakistan, she was assigned to work in a mental hospital. "After 3 months," she recalled, "I was completely discouraged." But she quickly added: "Then a Peace Corps 'evaluator' came to see how I was doing and pointed out the challenge."

Her conclusion: "I decided to stay. I haven't had a vacation since."

To identify herself more closely with the people, she adopted Pakistani dress. Her gentle persistence resulted in better treatment for the patients.

Examples like this are a reminder that courage and competence bolstered by God's grace are not lacking in the world. What this young woman has done, you too can do, with the Lord's help, in your own sphere of life.

❖

"Show yourself in all respects a model of good deeds." [TITUS 2:7]

❖

Help me, O Lord God, not only to be hopeful, but also to assist others to overcome their difficulties.

Watch the Little Things

A lighted cigarette falling into his lap caused one motorist in California plenty of trouble.

The startled man quickly stopped his car and jumped out to brush off his smouldering trousers.

Scarcely had he done so when his car began rolling backwards. After chasing it, he tried to get into the auto. Too late —it rolled over his foot and tumbled down an embankment.

Meanwhile, the lighted cigarette, wedged in the seat, kept on burning. Soon the entire auto was ablaze. Then in speedy succession the grass, a fence and a nearby woods caught fire.

Little mistakes seldom set off such a chain reaction of harmful effects. But you probably know from your own experience how much needless trouble can result from small beginnings.

Show foresight, with God's help, by nipping in the bud the little dangers that can injure others as well as yourself. Then you will prevent more than a few large problems.

❖

"He who is faithful in a very little is faithful also in much." [LUKE 16:10]

❖

Remind me, O divine Savior, that trifles can lead to perfection, but that perfection is no trifle.

To the World Through You

More than 7 centuries ago Francis of Assisi composed this prayer. It breathes a spirit of true charity that is needed today as much as it was in his own time:

"Lord, make me an instrument of Your peace.
Where there is hatred, let me sow love;
Where there is injury, pardon;
Where there is doubt, faith;
Where there is despair, hope;
Where there is darkness, light;
Where there is sadness, joy.
O, Divine Master, grant that I may not so much seek to be consoled as to console;
To be understood as to understand;
To be loved as to love;
For it is in giving that we receive;
It is in pardoning that we are pardoned;
It is in dying that we are born to eternal life."

Seek ways of your own to put this inspiring prayer to practice in everyday life and you are bound to leave the world better than you found it.

✧

"By this all men will know that you are My disciples, if you have love for one another."
[JOHN 13:35]

✧

Let me be an instrument of Your love, O Lord, in every possible way.

Advice for College Students

A harried college student sent this urgent telegram to his parents at home: "Am without funds or friends. Please help."

His father immediately wired back this 2-word gem of advice: "Make friends."

Too often we fall into the illusion of thinking that someone else should help us meet responsibilities that we ought to shoulder ourselves.

Even in situations in which we feel we have a right to the assistance of others, it may not be forthcoming. This is no excuse for dodging the effort of facing our obligations manfully.

By the grace of God, we can frequently surprise ourselves in discovering and putting to constructive use the deep-lying powers of mind, heart and soul that we never thought were there.

When recourse to outside help is impossible, make up your mind to "go with what you've got." But don't let your own success at "self-help" deter you from aiding others who reasonably look to you for assistance.

✧

"Admonish the idle, encourage the faint-hearted, help the weak, be patient with them all." [1 THESSALONIANS 5:14]

✧

Keep me ever mindful, O Lord, that even the most independent person would be nothing without You.

Unique Exercise for Indian Babies

The Navajo Indians' ancient practice of strapping their babies to cradle boards for as much as 20 hours a day forces the growing infant to use his muscles in a very effective way.

Although the baby's body seems to be practically motionless, it is constantly squirming and straining against the swaddling cloths that bind it tightly to the board.

As a result it strengthens its muscles as well as, if not better than, other children do through normal exercise.

Circumstances in your life that seem to "hem you in" and restrict your freedom of action can often be blessings in disguise.

By all means recognize the limitations of the many and varied situations in which you often find yourself. But don't let them frustrate or defeat you.

With God's help see in every hindrance a challenging opportunity to strengthen yourself in many valuable ways.

❖

"We know that in everything God works for good with those who love Him."
[ROMANS 8:28]

❖

Grant, O Holy Spirit, that we may profit by obstacles rather than be overcome by them.

A Frog on the Windshield

The two beady eyes of a frog proved too much for one distracted motorist. He ended up by crashing through a fence and knocking down a telephone pole.

As the 64-year-old man reported it: "I saw a head and two beady eyes looking at me through the window."

Upset by the unexpected intruder, which he took for a snake, he stepped on the gas pedal instead of the brake.

Apart from a wrecked car and property, the only fatality in the crash was the frog.

Unexpected interruptions can unsettle even the most skillful persons. Often they cannot be avoided.

However, vigilance in matters under one's control may often minimize difficulties before they get out of hand.

You owe it to God, your neighbor and yourself to anticipate trouble.

Take whatever steps may be necessary to avoid difficulties and you may be rendering a far greater service than you realize.

✧

"Blessed is the man who endures trial."
[JAMES 1:12]

✧

Enable me to do the best I can, O Father, while trusting in Your mercy.

Paint Job Done out of Spite

Waking up to find his house had been newly painted was almost too much for one man in Carlisle, England.

"I walked out the front door," he said, "and there it was, all painted pink."

He suspected a prankster and called police.

Upon investigation, the party involved turned out to be his landlord.

"I painted it pink at 5 o'clock in the morning," the owner readily admitted. "It's my house—I mean I own it—and I can do with it what I want to."

The strange situation grew out of a long-standing dispute between the two men over rent payment.

Most of us are tempted at times to allow spite to take the place of reason.

Besides failing to gain its objective, vindictiveness often boomerangs on the one who gives in to it. This is because God made us to give as well as to get.

Instead of becoming preoccupied with your own rights and feelings, have the largeness of heart to make room for the legitimate concerns of others.

✧

"Vengeance is Mine, I will repay, says the Lord." [ROMANS 12:19]

✧

Show me how to expand my outlook by generosity, O Lord, and not to narrow it by selfishness.

Two Inches of Water, but . . .

The following urgent rescue plea came to the police during a storm.

"Come immediately. I am in dire circumstances. I am standing in two inches of water."

"That isn't enough," replied the policeman.

"Yes, but I'm on the second floor," the frantic man pleaded.

Most of us have to make a lifelong fight against the tendency to overstate our own problems and underestimate those of others. The situation doesn't improve when those who look to us for aid fail to express themselves clearly.

But if you are motivated by a Christlike desire to be of service to all humanity, you will be surprised at your growing ability to evaluate and relieve the true needs of others.

Whether it is rescue from a storm, from bad housing or oppressive working conditions, opportunities to assist your fellow men will crowd your life—provided your eyes are open to see and grasp them.

✧

"Learn to do good; seek justice, correct oppression." [ISAIAH 1:17]

✧

May I see the smallness of my own difficulties, O Holy Spirit, and the magnitude of the needs of others.

Fork Went "Down the Hatch"

A pert young miss in Fort Worth, Texas, astonished doctors by inadvertently swallowing a dinner fork.

The 21-year-old blonde was sitting in a coffee shop telling a friend about her tonsils when her troubles began.

"I was holding my tongue down with the fork handle," she explained. "I got to laughing and it just went down."

After surgeons removed the utensil from her stomach, one hospital attendant called it the largest item he had ever heard of anyone swallowing.

"I still don't see how she did it," he marvelled.

"It was easy," the young woman blushed.

While a fork goes well with food, it should not go with it all the way to the stomach. A good thing in the wrong place suddenly becomes a bad thing because harmony is upset.

God made us in such a way that we will be happy and make others so only if right order reigns in our thoughts, desires and actions.

✧

"But all things should be done decently and in order."   [1 CORINTHIANS 14:40]

✧

Give me the insight, O Holy Spirit, always to respect Your ways, whether I fully understand them or not.

One Shovel Cuts Off Europe

Dozens of telephone conversations between London and Europe came to an abrupt end when a workman dug a hole outside Bert's Cafe in Swanley, England.

As he operated his mechanical shovel on a drain site, he little realized that he was severing thousands of connections on the continental cable. International telephone links were thrown into confusion.

"Where I am told to dig I just dig," the workman later said in defense of himself. "No one told me to look out for a cable."

After a delay of 10 hours, phone calls to Europe were resumed, Eurovision's TV was back in action and Early Bird satellite communications between Britain and the Continent were again in operation.

In carrying out instructions of any kind, God expects each of us to use good judgment and common sense.

If our decisions are based on divine truth and love as well as sound human principles, there is little chance that we will act carelessly or blindly.

✧

"Let us not love in word or speech but in deed and truth."   [1 JOHN 3:18]

✧

Endow me, O Holy Spirit, with good sense in fulfilling Your divine laws.

Behind the Daring of Columbus

On August 3, 1492, Christopher Columbus and his fleet of three tiny ships lifted anchor in Palos, Portugal, and started westward on a long and dangerous voyage.

Conditions aboard the little vessels were far from ideal. The usual diet was salt meat, which often became rancid, and dried peas with a little wine and water.

Time and again the frightened sailors tried to persuade Columbus to return. They were on the verge of mutiny just before the first glimpse of the New World was finally sighted on the morning of October 12.

Behind the big vision and daring faith that carried Christopher Columbus through every heartbreaking obstacle was the conviction that he was a Christ-bearer serving God's purpose and the well-being of all men.

If you wish to leave the world better than you found it, you, too, must pay the price of suffering. But for all eternity you will rejoice in the fact that you, too, were a Christ-bearer.

✧

"For as we share abundantly in Christ's sufferings, so through Christ we share abundantly in comfort too."   [2 CORINTHIANS 1:5]

✧

Help me, O Holy Spirit, to brave all difficulties to achieve the goal You have set for me.

Prize-Winning Boy Gets Bored

An 11-year-old who was the outstanding scholar in his class used to become so bored outside school that he ran away from home 10 times in one year.

When police brought him home after his latest absence, his mother could only say: "I think his brain is so active, he goes off like this to give it a rest."

Most parents do not have to cope with a restless genius. But, no matter what a child's mental capacity may be, it is up to his father and mother to recognize his hidden potential, carefully cultivate it and then give it constructive direction.

A youngster who is trained and guided in this manner seldom bores himself or the people around him.

By failing to help young people develop their talents, we may stunt their growth, shortchange others and inadvertently let them drift into trouble.

In a very real way, the future of mankind depends on how adults foster and direct the bit of greatness that God has entrusted to every child.

✧

"Train up a child in the way he should go, and when he is old he will not depart from it."
[PROVERBS 22:6]

✧

O Lord, give us the wisdom to deal with children as You would.

Eviction Comes for a Lion

Lions belong in jungles or zoos, and not in the home, officials of one Pennsylvania township ruled.

The animal in question, a full-grown 300-pounder, was frequently to be seen riding in the front seat of a tow truck driven by its owner.

Neighbors of the man, disturbed by the proximity of an unchained king of the jungle, signed a petition asking that the beast be banished.

Officials agreed to the request and took action to have the lion moved to safer quarters.

Some of us may need to be reminded at times that our own recreations or hobbies must be limited because of the inconvenience they may cause others.

A person who is preoccupied with self stands little chance of understanding this basic point. One who embraces God and others will grasp it without being told.

Do more than steer clear of harm. God expects you to make every reasonable effort to bring kindness, encouragement and inspiration into the lives of all you meet.

✧

"That is, that we may be mutually encouraged
by each other's faith, both yours and mine."
[ROMANS 1:12]

✧

Let me be more concerned with what I can
give to the world, O Lord, instead of what I
can get out of it.

The Nearly Perfect Pearl

Pearl divers almost made the discovery of a lifetime while fishing in the waters off West Africa.

After bringing up hundreds of oysters with small pearls or none at all, the divers found a gigantic one with a pearl the size of a pigeon's egg in it.

The jubilant captain of the fleet estimated the pearl's worth at $100,000.

On cleaning the oyster's shell before chipping out the precious find, however, he detected a marine worm that had bored a microscopic hole from the outside of the shell. It went through the heart of the pearl, rendering it completely worthless.

Too many individuals who could be of tremendous value, in God's plan, to the welfare of humanity, are prevented by a similar tragic flaw from achieving their true potential.

Don't let pride, carelessness or material comforts block your innate powers. Seek divine assistance in preserving your integrity. In the long run, you will attain the "pearl of great price."

❖

*"On finding one pearl of great value, he went
and sold all that he had and bought it."*
[MATTHEW 13:46]

❖

Keep me from being misdirected, Lord, by any personal fault, small or large.

Before Success Goes Work

Queen Victoria sought to compliment the celebrated pianist, Ignace Paderewski, by saying: "Mr. Paderewski, you are a genius!"

He immediately replied: "Perhaps, Your Majesty, but before I was a genius, I was a drudge."

The great Michelangelo echoed the same thought when he said: "If people knew how hard I have had to work to gain my mastery, it wouldn't seem wonderful at all."

The story behind most people who have achieved any success in life, be it as a good homemaker, a capable statesman, an outstanding artist or a canonized saint, is usually one of hard work.

And invariably it is the type of work that involves an endless expenditure of time and labor, often done in solitude, and with little or no appreciation on the part of others.

If you would make a true success of your life for time and for eternity, never forget that it will be achieved by your willingness to make countless efforts that will be known only to God.

✧

"Whatever good any one does, he will receive the same again from the Lord."
[EPHESIANS 6:8]

✧

Keep me reminded, O Savior, that I am here to work my way to heaven.

A Cup of Tea Changed Things

Upon investigating a loud crash at 5 o'clock one morning outside her house in Spalding, England, a woman was horrified to find that a 23-ton truck had smashed into the front of her cottage.

She quickly recovered from her shock, however, and did what any British housewife would do in the circumstances. She made a cup of tea for the truck driver.

"I am sorry I have no milk," she apologized.

"That's all right," the driver replied, "there are 3,000 gallons on your doorstep."

Under the most upsetting or aggravating circumstances, it is possible to ease a difficult situation by a word or deed of thoughtfulness.

One person like you can accomplish much even if you do no more than lessen tensions in the family circle, at school or on the job.

God will bless you if you strive to make a bad situation a little better rather than ignore or worsen it.

✧

"If God has so loved us, we ought to love one another."　　　　　[JOHN 4:11]

✧

Let me show compassion for those in trouble, O Lord.

Sound Waves Save Boy's Eye

A quarter-inch piece of brass was removed from the left eye of an 8-year-old boy in a first-of-its-kind operation. It was done by sonar, or bouncing sound.

A chip from a brass cartridge that the youngster was playing with had lodged in his eye, damaging the lens.

Because brass is non-magnetic, the fragment could not be lifted out by usual methods. Fearing it might corrode and necessitate removal of the entire eye, doctors at Walter Reed Hospital in Washington, D.C., decided to use the sonar method. It had been tried on animals, but never on a human being.

The operating surgeon used a small oscilloscope with an echoing device that located the piece of brass hidden in the eye, much as submarines are detected by sonar. Tiny extractors lifted it out.

Medical science is continually discovering new ways to protect man's health. Pray that many capable young men and women will dedicate their lives to curing the mental and physical ills of mankind.

✧

"I was sick and you visited Me."

[MATTHEW 25:26]

✧

O divine Physician, bless all those who strive
valiantly to overcome man's infirmities.

Human Flame Thrower Gets in Trouble

A fire-eater in Paris found himself in jail for 2 months because he belched flames at a newspaper stand.

The man attracted a group of commuters by swallowing fire in front of the Montparnasse train station.

But a nearby vendor thought the "artist" was getting too close to her stand for safety. She shouted at him: "Get out of here. You'll burn my papers. Go away or I'll call the police."

This offended the fire-eater who quickly retorted by spewing flame at the stand. Police arrested him for burning a stack of 150 newspapers.

When we give vent to hurt feelings, nothing but trouble usually results. A bad situation is simply worsened.

Let your heart be filled with the fire of love and then you will be sure that its flame will always warm but never burn.

Cultivate a love for people that is rooted in love of God and you will develop the divine art of decreasing problems for others rather than increasing them.

✧

"Make love your aim, and earnestly desire the spiritual gifts." [1 CORINTHIANS 14:1]

✧

Instill in me, O Father, the same love for all men that You have for me.

What One Person Can Do

One man who couldn't vote himself was instrumental in convincing hundreds of others to go to the polls.

The 43-year-old man, a Cuban refugee, placed a table outside his small grocery store in New York to remind passers-by of their obligation.

In addition, he provided copies of the State literacy test for residents to study before they go to register. A sign in his window gave the address and the hours of the local place of registry.

"You have to vote in order to have the kind of government you want," his wife explained. "My husband is in love with democracy but he isn't a citizen and can't vote."

Then she added: "So he's trying to get others to vote for him. He feels that is his contribution to the American government."

Such an example speaks volumes. Our liberty is given by God, but it will not be maintained without our active co-operation.

Your vote is a foundation-stone of freedom.

✧

"For you were called to freedom."
[GALATIANS 5:13]

✧

Guide me, O Lord, to look upon voting as
a serious obligation and tremendous privilege.

Refuses to Wait for Freight Train

Tired of waiting for a slow freight train to pass, a driver in Louisville, Ky., uncoupled the cars and drove his truck through.

What he didn't know was that a patrolman was watching him, scarcely believing his eyes.

The impatient truck driver was fined $100 on the unusual charge of "uncoupling a moving train."

We are all tempted to resort to short cuts when our own desires are thwarted. But before taking a hasty or ill-considered step, we should ask ourselves some searching questions.

For example, does my action coincide with God's law, or does it ignore one of His basic precepts?

Does it express my love for others, or does it cut me off from my fellow men?

Is my action something I would do in the full light of day, or is it something I would perform only if it were not discovered by others?

You need never fear if both your goals and means are honorable.

❖

"He who is noble devises noble things, and by noble things he stands." [ISAIAH 32:8]

❖

Inspire me to have noble aims, Holy Spirit, and to accomplish them in a spirit of service.

Good Reason for Calm

A woman passenger on her first trans-Atlantic voyage became more and more frightened as the ship pitched and tossed in one of the worst storms of the season.

Catching sight of the Captain as he was hurrying back to the bridge, she dashed up to him and frantically asked:

"Captain, Captain, what's going to happen?"

Seeing that the nervous woman needed reassurance on her first storm experience at sea, the Captain tried to give her the best reason possible for keeping calm.

"Don't worry, Madam," he said, "after all, we are in the hands of God."

"Oh!" she gasped. "Is it as bad as that?"

During the voyage through life, each of us is bound to encounter storms that bewilder and often terrify us.

But no matter how hopeless and forbidding the outlook may seem, you can maintain an inner calm that no tempest can entirely upset.

You can always take consolation in the fact that the Lord Who made you loves you so much that He will never abandon you in fair weather or foul.

❖

"I fear no evil; for You are with me."
[PSALM 23:4]

❖

Thanks to You, O divine Savior, for watching over us in fair weather and foul.

305

Champion of India's Poor

The dedication of a frail little man has provided millions of acres of land for India's poor.

Since 1951 Vinoba Bhave has walked tirelessly throughout India persuading wealthy landowners to give some of their property to their impoverished countrymen.

Ambassador B. K. Nehru, as he accepted in New York City an award from the Family of Man Society on Bhave's behalf, said:

"Bhave is no politician nor does he even lay claim to statesmanship. He has proved beyond doubt that love can overcome lust for wealth and that moral suasion can be employed to persuade the rich to share their riches with the poor."

Then he added: "A far-reaching revolution by consent, of deep philosophical significance, has been wrought by Vinoba Bhave . . . He is proving that the greatest social changes can be worked by love and not by violence."

One person, armed only with intense love for God and his fellow man, can move the hearts of thousands by single-mindedly pursuing his ideal.

✧

"Reap the fruit of steadfast love."
[HOSEA 10:12]

✧

Let me never underestimate, Lord, the good results that come from active trust in You.

How to Tame an Angry Rhino

A fight between a troublesome rhinoceros and a startled condor brought 8 firemen and 6 policemen to a zoo in Southampton, England.

The trouble started as the 2,000-pound rhino was being led to a specially reinforced crate for shipment to a zoo in Germany.

The huge animal lumbered against the cage of "Conrad the Condor" and the bird angrily flapped its 10-foot wings. The enraged rhinoceros defied all efforts to maneuver him into the crate.

To the rescue came a veterinarian with a hypodermic needle loaded with a powerful sedative. After one injection the rhino fell peacefully asleep and soon was aboard a ship for Hanover, Germany.

It is as important to know how to achieve solutions as it is to have good intentions.

By attention to detail and constant application, you can strive for the degree of competence God wishes you to have in meeting your personal, family and career responsibilities.

✧

"Whatever your hand finds to do, do it with your might."   [ECCLESIASTES 9:10]

✧

Help me to meet my obligations with hope, determination and skill, O Jesus.

More Than Matches Needed

Setting fire to the local brewery was one housewife's way of trying to stop her husband's drinking.

The angry woman gave police this oversimplified explanation: "If the brewery burns down and they don't make beer, my husband can't drink."

Damage to the brewery was estimated at $62,000.

Many a good person, exasperated by failure in high places or low, jumps to the conclusion that abuses can be cured by one sweep of the hand—or a few matches.

But such impatience usually compounds the trouble instead of bringing about the desired remedy.

Be alert to weaknesses in persons and institutions. But be realistic at the same time in trying to reclaim sinners or correct long-standing abuses.

Make haste slowly in replacing evil with good. Distinguish between the wheat and the chaff.

In short, imitate the Divine Redeemer in finding the element of hope and building on that.

✧

"Do not be overcome by evil, but overcome evil with good." [ROMANS 12:21]

✧

Give me both the vision and patience, O loving Savior, to right what is wrong.

People Rush to Pay Bills

More than 50 residents frantically trying to pay overdue water bills suddenly descended on the City Hall of Miami Springs, Fla.

"I never saw anything like it," one clerk said. "They came dashing in as fast as they could, with the money in their hands."

Officials saw no apparent reason for the sudden arrival of such a large group, until they learned that a road grading machine had accidentally cut a main water line. The residents were unaware of what had happened and attributed the lack of water to their own delinquency in paying bills.

The very fact that these conscience-stricken people made a hurried effort to pay their bills is a hopeful sign in itself. It is tacit evidence that they were aware of their obligations even when they were slow in living up to them.

Encourage the latent goodness that God has instilled in every person and you will do far more than help people pay their water bills on time.

✧

*"Let us consider how to stir up one another
to love and good works."*   [HEBREWS 10:24]

✧

Let me focus attention on what is good in man, O Lord, as well as recognize his failings.

Small Town Does a Big Job

The town that "wouldn't take no for an answer" might be one way to describe Deer River, Minn.

Some years ago the town, with a population of 1,000, was forced to close its small hospital because it was a fire hazard. Even though Deer River was known as a "depressed area," the businessmen, farmers and other citizens determined to have a new one.

State and federal funds were not made available so they began raising the $275,000 they needed. Everybody pitched in and in 3 years they had enough to start building. Then, admiring this grass roots initiative, a small foundation and the state legislature provided additional funds on a matching basis.

In its first 15 months of operation, the 20-bed hospital had cared for more than 1,000 persons. In all, it services 5,000 in the neighboring area.

Personal responsibility and individual initiative have always been the hallmark of those who wish to serve their fellow man for the love of God. It may not be easy but the reward far outweighs whatever efforts are involved.

✧

"Let us rise up and build." [NEHEMIAH 2:18]

✧

Never let me lose heart, O Lord, in any endeavor that will result in benefit for others.

The Real Meaning of "Candidate"

Do you know the origin of the word candidate?

The term comes from *"candidatus,"* meaning clothed in white. The root Latin word *"candere"* signifies to shine with a penetrating whiteness as a candle does in the dark.

In ancient days candidates for the Roman Senate donned a pure white toga, which had been rubbed in white chalk until it gleamed. This specially whitened toga was the distinguishing mark of a person seeking public office. It signified that his past record merited future confidence.

Keep this lofty ideal ever in mind and you will encourage those with outstanding ability and integrity to represent you in government.

Don't become cynical when some persons in public affairs fail to live up to their noble trust. Make an even greater effort to find candidates who shine with the inner glow of conscience as well as the "outer whiteness" that should distinguish every office-holder.

✧

"If we walk in the light, as He is in the light, we have fellowship with one another."

[1 JOHN 1:7]

✧

Bless, O Lord, those in government who strive conscientiously to serve the good of all.

Benjamin Franklin's Big Vision

When he died in 1790 Benjamin Franklin left $6,000 to his native Boston. He stipulated that the city lend the money at 5 per cent interest to "young married artificers."

The original small fund steadily increased in value over the years. Now it has a market value of more than $2 million in cash, stocks and bonds. In the next 25 years it is expected to double in value.

Franklin's will specified that in 1991 the fund should be split, with 74 per cent going to the state of Massachusetts and the balance to the city of Boston. The fund will then be worth an estimated 5½ million dollars.

Persons who are blessed with long range vision, a high sense of purpose and a keen appreciation of the far-reaching potential of small beginnings usually leave the world better than they found it.

Put to good use whatever talent God has entrusted to you in small ways and large. You may one day be surprised at how much good you can accomplish.

❖

"Whatever good the Lord will do to us, the same will we do to you." [NUMBERS 10:32]

❖

Teach me, O Jesus, to see big possibilities for good in the smallest opportunities.

Blind Man Climbs over Roof Tops

A building wrecker, who has been blind for 31 years, looks like any other workman when he climbs around roof tops in Columbus, Ohio.

Despite his handicap, the sightless man can walk on beams or wield a hammer or crowbar as well as any of his fellow workers. In 18 years he has helped demolish more than 2,000 buildings.

The only concession the blind building wrecker makes to his disability is the cane he carries on the job.

If a person deprived of sight can accomplish such things, how much more should be achieved by those who are blessed with all their faculties.

Don't sit back and find excuses for yourself because of some minor or imaginary handicap. Instead, show reasonable determination and daring in meeting the challenges that God presents to you every day.

You will live a fuller, richer life if you put all your capabilities to work rather than leave them undeveloped.

✧

"Put out into the deep, and let down your nets for a catch." [LUKE 5:4]

✧

May I use well the talent You have entrusted to me, O Lord.

The Pigeons That Didn't Go Home

Homing pigeons—213 of them—fooled everybody during a race in Japan. They got lost.

In all, 217 birds took off from an island 190 miles off the coast and headed for Tokyo, but only 4 ever arrived.

"We're flabbergasted," exclaimed a spokesman. "They're long overdue. But it simply isn't conceivable that all 213 were lost or were assaulted by enemies of the sky."

It isn't too often that so many homing pigeons "fly the coop." But when persons we depend upon to fulfill responsibilities fail to measure up, the consequences are likely to be serious.

Rather than waste valuable time lamenting the shortcomings of others, look into yourself to make sure that you are living up to your own obligations to God, self and neighbor.

Then you will be in a better position to spur others to doing what is expected of them. And you will be winging in the right direction.

✧

"How can you say to your brother, 'Let me take the speck out of your eye,' when there is the log in your own eye?" [MATTHEW 7:4]

✧

Keep me ever aware, Holy Spirit, of my responsibilities and enable me to carry them out faithfully.

Gallant Death in Bus Terminal

A man paid a high price for going to the aid of 3 teenage girls being mistreated by 2 drunken young men. He was stabbed to death by one of the men after walking over to them and saying: "Why don't you leave these girls alone?"

The slaying took place in the heart of the business district of Jamaica, Long Island.

"This man came to our rescue. He was a real hero," said one of the girls afterwards. "When we asked him to help us, he did. One of the men who was pestering us was twisting my arm . . . I asked 3 other passengers to help . . . but they just kept on walking."

Then she added: "It's horrible to think he had to die. What bothers me is that he needn't have died if other people had helped him when I asked them to."

Even one person sacrificing his life in such a way gives witness that every man is capable of heroic love as well as deadly hatred. God leaves the decision to each of us. But what we do—or neglect to do—affects everyone for better or for worse.

✧

"By this we know love, that He laid down His life." [1 JOHN 3:16]

✧

May we learn, O Redeemer, how to prove our love for You by befriending those in trouble.

315

If His Wife Had Voted

One man will never again tell his wife not to vote. The individual in question happened to be a candidate running for his third term in the Georgia House of Representatives.

Feeling sure that he would not have any opposition, he assured his wife that it wasn't necessary for her to go to the polls.

But little did he bargain for a spur-of-the-moment write-in vote in his district. His opponent fared so well that the final results showed a surprising 254–254 tie.

It is difficult to realize how important it is for every person to be intelligent and constant in protecting the blessings of freedom.

You can see for yourself how disastrous the "my vote doesn't count" attitude could be if everybody thought and acted that way.

Point out to all you can reach that each of us owes it to God, country and mankind to fulfill the obligations that accompany the blessings of peace and freedom.

✧

"Choose wise, understanding, and experienced men." [DEUTERONOMY 1:13]

✧

Thanks to You, O Father of all, for the many privileges of freedom.

Pilot's Singing Soothes Angry Lion

A new method of lion-taming was hastily developed by a pilot who had crashed in rugged California mountains. Stepping from the wreckage of his plane, the flyer was confronted by an angry mountain lion.

On an impulse, the frightened man called out "Shalom" (the Hebrew word for peace and goodwill). To his surprise, the lion calmed down a bit. Then he began to sing—gauging each song's effect by the way the animal's tail twitched.

After some success with French and German songs, and noticeable irritation when he tried "rock 'n' roll," the pilot tried Hebrew songs. "It seemed as though a smile ran over his face," he commented later.

Help arrived just as the appreciative lion began to tire of the impromptu concert.

Don't wait until you are in a tight spot to begin promoting peace among persons who are hostile. You may be met with indifference, rebuffs or open opposition. But your imitation of the Prince of Peace will bring an eventual share in His eternal joy.

✧

"Seek peace and pursue it." [1 PETER 3:11]

✧

Lord, make me an instrument of Your peace.

"Funeral" Pleases Living Grandmother

A grandmother in Samoa attended her own funeral and enjoyed every minute of it.

"This was a wonderful funeral," she exclaimed, "and the happiest day of my life."

The 74-year-old woman took part in an old tribal custom called "the funeral for the living."

It was given by her son, the chief, who ordered the ceremony as a token of his love and respect.

The festivities included a big dinner and an exchange of gifts with friends and relatives.

There is endless variety in the ways by which people of different backgrounds show affection for their loved ones. But, however expressed, it all adds up to the same thing.

This universal testimony to respect for parents among all peoples of the world is based on gratitude for the gift of life.

It should likewise lead us to a sense of reverence for the wider human family—for we are all brothers under the same loving Father.

✧

"In Him we live and move and have our being."   [ACTS 17:28]

✧

Make me a champion, Father, of the rights of man by prayer, word and positive deeds.

n *Woman Hailed for Mercy*

cently
He at-
n him.
ld his
e sent

rd stu-

nded,"
o read
a po-

and 3
somed

od has
ut the

lliterate young woman in Madras, India,
nal award for giving a striking example of
service.

s a brick-carrier for 60 cents a day, the
ame upon 2 motorcyclists lying in a pool
; main road.

ds passed them by, she put down her
:arched for a taxi to bring them to a
drivers refused to take the injured men,

id that the incident showed that educa-
ot automatically make a person a better

nented, "the quality of crusading mercy
a humble heart."

lity of mercy" is hidden in every heart.
there. But He depends on man to dis-
his fellow man.

enteredness or fear of involvement by
ind all.

✧

*hese three, do you think, proved
he man who fell among the rob-*
[LUKE 10:36]

✧

courage, Lord, to take some risks
; to the needs of others.

Backward Student Wins Scholarship

A teenager who consistently failed his examinations r
won a mathematics scholarship to Oxford University.
tributed his achievement to the faith one teacher had

Most of the 16-year-old boy's other instructors had
parents that his future was dim and that he should
to an institution for retarded children.

One teacher, however, decided to give the backw;
dent special tests for children unable to read.

"We discovered that he was left-eyed and right-h;
the educator said. "This accounted for his inability
properly. We realized that the boy was no fool—bu
tential genius."

After spending 2 hours a day on remedial reading
hours on mathematics and science, the youngster blo
into a scholar within a few years.

Help others to discover and develop the abilities C
entrusted to them. It requires much time and effort,
results reach into eternity.

❖

*"Let each of you look not only to his own
interests, but also to the interests of others."*
[PHILIPPIANS 2:4]

❖

Enlighten me, O Holy Spirit, in my efforts to
bring out the hidden power in myself and
others.

Finder of Lost Dog Declines Reward

A lost terrier, called Pretzel, meant so much to one man and his family that they put an ad in their local newspaper. They offered as a reward their station wagon and $400—all the money they had in the bank—for its return.

A gas station attendant saw the ad and thought the dog he found wandering at a bus stop might be Pretzel.

On checking he realized he had the lost dog. When he returned it to the distraught owners, they tried to give the finder the promised recompense.

But seeing their joy was reward enough for the man. He gallantly declined the station wagon and money, and then added: "If Pretzel ever has puppies, I'd like one for my 3 children."

All too few people experience the deep happiness that results from trying to solve the problems, small or large, of those in trouble. And yet it is a divine paradox that we find our own true fulfillment by entering in a Christ-like way into the difficulties of others.

✧

"Rejoice with those who rejoice, weep with those who weep."   [ROMANS 12:15]

✧

Teach me, O Holy Spirit, to discover my better self by showing a concern for the needs of others.

Praise Is Appreciation

Praise is one of the most frequently used terms in the Bible. In the Book of Psalms alone it occurs 74 times.

The dictionary defines the verb "praise" as: "to express approbation; to commend; to glorify, especially God, by homage."

It is derived from the Latin verb "pretiare," meaning "to prize—to have an appreciation for."

Xenophon in 360 B.C. was hardly exaggerating when he said: "The sweetest of all sounds is praise."

"True praise roots and spreads," observed George Herbert in 1629.

However, as the great Augustine warned in 400 A.D., "Falsely praising a person is lying."

If praise is based on a true appreciation then it must be sincere. And if appreciation should grow according to the greatness of the person addressed, then the Hebrew Psalmist shows the way for all by reserving his joyous cries of praise for Him Who made heaven and earth:

✧

"*Let everything that breathes praise the Lord.*"   [PSALM 150:6]

✧

Let my thoughts, words and actions, O Father, always be directed to Your greater honor and glory.

That Others May Have Food

A retired professor is hard at work trying to get much more food out of tropical soils than is now obtained.

A few years ago the professor emeritus of Cornell College of Agriculture, 70, went with his wife, a retired nutritionist, to the Philippines. He believes that yields of rice can often be doubled and even quadrupled by the use of improved varieties and cultural practices.

The enthusiastic professor did five years of work with the International Rice Research Institute in the Philippines. He succeeded in growing crops of rice, sweet potatoes and sweet corn on the same land in less than 12 months. Now he is working on ways to grow rice with less labor, by direct seeding into dry soil mechanically.

Greater progress can be made in solving the world's hunger problems if tens of thousands of competent persons make it their business to provide the adequate food that all men need and that God wishes them to have.

✧

"Share your bread with the hungry."

[ISAIAH 58:7]

✧

Inspire those with the needed ability, Holy Spirit, to search for ways to feed the hungry.

Many Amputees Benefit from One Man

More than 6,000 disabled people in Mexico have benefited by the compassion of one individual. He had learned the value of rehabilitation when he lost his own leg in an auto accident.

During his recovery, the man was impressed by the problems of amputees. So he enlisted the aid of individuals, companies and the government to set up a rehabilitation center in Mexico City.

The hospital takes care of 90 per cent of its patients free. Of the 6,500 treated, 95 per cent have learned to use artificial limbs so well that they can resume normal activities in whole or in part.

The sale of articles produced by the patients themselves has made the operation self-supporting.

Give thanks for God's benefits to you by seeing that they are made available to those less well off.

To do this is to frankly acknowledge that all good things —material, intellectual and spiritual—come from the Lord and are destined to be used for His glory.

✧

"For from Him and through Him and to Him are all things. To Him be glory forever."
[ROMANS 11:36]

✧

Grant me some of Your divine compassion, O Lord, that I may share with others.

Weighty Words from a Comedian

Turning to serious matters, humorist Sam Levenson recently expressed his thoughts on responsibility to a group of high school students.

From his own 20 years' experience as a public school teacher, Mr. Levenson said:

"Ours is a democracy of limited freedom, not total freedom. This is not a society free for anyone to do what he pleases, when he pleases.

"He must recognize the rights of others.

"We each have our limits and limitations.

"We need to play, but we must limit our playfulness. We must discipline ourselves and through discipline we will attain genuine freedom.

"Otherwise, doing as you please becomes anarchy and barbarism."

Exercise your freedom, which is one of God's most precious gifts, with due regard for the rights of others. Then you will be far more likely to achieve the liberty that only an untroubled conscience can give.

✣

"Live as free men, yet without using your freedom as a pretext for evil; but live as servants of God." [1 PETER 2:16]

✣

Grant me the grace, O Holy Spirit, to restrain my impulses when they may be harmful to others.

Making Bitter Sweet

One way to take the tartness out of even a lemon is first to eat a special African berry. Known as miracle fruit, it grows chiefly in the area from Ghana to the Congo.

It not only sweetens sour foods, but it also gives them a flavor that a natural or synthetic sweetener does not provide.

Widespread use of the wonder fruit may even open a new approach to dieting since it does not add caloric value as sugar does.

Shaped like a small football and less than an inch long, the berry grows on a large shrub, 6 to 15 feet high. Small amounts of pulp responsible for the sweetness are contained in the plant's large seeds.

Would that the human disposition could be sweetened in such a quick, effective way. Still it is within the power of every one of us by the grace of God to inject a pleasant note into the most unpalatable situations—to be gracious and forgiving when it would be so easy to be gruff and vindictive.

❖

"Be kind to one another, tenderhearted, forgiving one another." [EPHESIANS 4:32]

❖

Teach me, O loving Savior, to sweeten life, not make it more bitter.

Why Swindlers Succeed

After a swindler persuaded a woman to invest her life savings in a worthless project, she went to the Better Business Bureau with her tale of woe.

A sympathetic official, after explaining how difficult it would be to recover the money, asked: "But why didn't you come to us for advice before you got involved? Obviously you knew about our service."

"Yes, I knew all right," the victim admitted, "but I was afraid if I told you what I intended to do you would tell me not to do it."

We hurt our own best interests—and those of others, too —by thinking in a careless or contradictory manner.

God has endowed each of us with an intellect and free will. But He leaves it to us to put these noble faculties to work in a practical manner, not to neglect or misuse them.

In times of frustration or temptation, make a special effort to heed the warnings of your better judgment, and you will seldom have any regrets.

✧

"Reason is the beginning of every work, and counsel precedes every undertaking."
[SIRACH 37:16]

✧

Imbue me with the good sense, O Holy Spirit, to overcome my weaknesses.

Strength in Weakness

A woman's telephone call for help was so muffled that the police hurried to the wrong address.

When they did find the right house, she was grateful but assured them that the strangler had run off, probably when he heard the approach of the officers.

"Don't feel bad about getting the wrong address," she remarked. "You see, he was choking me when I called and I couldn't speak very clearly."

Coolness in the presence of danger is probably more an acquired trait than an inborn one.

Although it can proceed from a blind fatalism, it is most effective when based on an intelligent appraisal of any situation in the light of God's merciful design.

Rather than passively accept evils, abuses or injustices, especially when they affect others, take an active hand in setting them aright. Don't panic, but let your daring be tempered by prudence.

✧

"Take no part in the unfruitful works of darkness, but instead expose them."
[EPHESIANS 5:11]

✧

Keep me, O Lord, from running away from hardships, and grant me the strength to confront them manfully.

Shoulder Your Responsibilities

The really big problems that plague mankind today seldom come "out of the blue."

They happen because one person after another relinquishes that portion of leadership, however small, which in the divine plan each individual can and should contribute.

A large advertisement underlined the weakness in this approach when it pointed out that "soon there isn't anybody else left. Everybody is on that selfish bandwagon. And then it's you who pick up the check for your own past self-indulgence."

The ad concluded: "It's you who have to carry the same responsibility you thought you were shifting to other shoulders."

The difficulties, crises and issues that confront humanity today cannot be "swept under the rug."

They will be with us until enough persons, inspired by love of God and other men, confront them hopefully, decisively and constructively.

✧

"Aim at righteousness, faith, love and peace."
[2 TIMOTHY 2:22]

✧

Rather than expect others to provide benefits for me, O Lord, inspire me to do something for them.

The Compassion of a Hunting Guide

A Canadian hunting guide dropped everything to enable a Cleveland policeman to reach the bedside of his stricken father shortly before he died.

The policeman was deep in the Canadian woods on a bear hunt when he received news of his father's illness. He was about to give up hope of reaching his father's bedside—1,000 miles away—in time.

Then the guide, whom he had known for only 2 days, offered to help. He insisted on leaving his job, his wife and his 4-year-old daughter to make the 14-hour drive. He refused any money for his services.

"I've never met a more wonderful man," the officer remarked afterwards. "If there were more people with his humanitarianism, we would have none of the problems we have today."

Those who have the love of others in their hearts can, by the power of God, reach out from practically any situation to change the world for the better.

❖

"Love one another earnestly from the heart."
[1 PETER 1:22]

❖

Let me be alert and ready at any time, Lord, to come to the aid of anyone who may need me.

Strength Comes from Within

A professional strongman amazed onlookers by pulling a 156,000-pound railroad car 176 feet in 30 seconds.

He did this as a group of workers in the Pennsylvania Railroad's yards in New York trotted alongside of him and chanted "Go, go, go."

Afterwards, while the veins in his forehead were still protruding from the strain, he calmly put the rope he had used back into his brown leather bag.

Then he said happily: "This is the peak of my career. After this, I'm going back to keeping airplanes from taking off and to lifting elephants."

The 34-year-old strongman claims to have prevented a 2-motor plane from getting off the ground. He also insists he delights in lifting baby elephants.

While physical prowess has its advantages, the kind of strength that is independent of muscle power comes from within and should grow with age.

If you ask the Lord for the power to bear adversity and even to help carry the burdens of others, He will grant it to you in the measure you need.

✧

"Comfort those who are in any affliction with the comfort with which we ourselves are comforted by God."   [2 CORINTHIANS 1:4]

✧

Let me strive for the strength, O Lord, that never grows old and the power that never diminishes.

Youngster Saves His Family

A 10-year-old raced 4 times into his burning home in Lake-wood, N.J., and rescued his 5 brothers and sisters from the flames.

The blaze was started by a 2-year-old playing with matches.

The young hero, whose parents were away at the time, raced across the street to tell a neighbor: "My house is on fire, mister! Call the fire department."

Instead of waiting for help, he rushed into the house to carry out his 2-month-old brother. Then he lifted his year-old sister and led the others to safety.

"There's no doubt about it," the police chief said later, "the boy saved all their lives."

Knowing what to do in an emergency is one thing; actually carrying it out can be quite another.

When situations arise that call for quick action, seek assistance from those best equipped to give it. But don't stop there. You may unlock surprising powers, with the Lord's help, if you do what you can without delay.

✧

"Seek advice from every wise man, and do not despise any useful counsel." [TOBIT 4:18]

✧

Strengthen my will, O Jesus, to move quickly when the good of others depends on it.

Risks Life for $14

A homeless laborer risked being crushed to death under a London subway in order to regain a 5-pound note.

The man had been clutching the money in his hand while waiting for a train. A sudden gust of wind blew the bill out of his fingers and onto the tracks.

The unexpected loss of his money so disconcerted the workman that he jumped down to the tracks, just as a train raced into the station. Before it could be braked to a stop, 3 cars had roared over him.

Fearing the worst, the station master crawled under the train expecting to find the man no longer among the living. But he was happily surprised to see him sitting in the safety pit, dirty and bruised, but with his 5-pound note clutched tightly in his hand.

Men will take dangerous risks to protect or recover material treasures. So should you be willing to endure much to guard or restore the spiritual treasure that endures through the endless years of eternity.

✧

"Lay up for yourselves treasures in heaven, where neither moth nor rust consumes and where thieves do not break in and steal."
[MATTHEW 6:20]

✧

Sharpen my sense of values, O Lord, so that I may always keep first things first.

He Took the Wrong Baby

One man got so irritated at a gathering of young couples that he started to leave with somebody else's baby.

"Get your coat," he snapped to his wife, "I'll take the baby. We're leaving."

As he hurried towards the door with infant in arms, another guest shouted: "Wait, wait!"

"No," he growled. "We're going."

"Well, I hate to see you go," the other man calmly replied. "But you'll have to wait a minute anyhow. You've got my baby."

How often the innocent suffer when a person gives vent to his annoyance! Indulging in temper tantrums usually makes a bad situation even more complicated.

You have much to gain and nothing to lose if you strive to disagree without being disagreeable.

Blend firmness with kindness and gentleness when you must take exception. You will surprise yourself to learn how effective an instrument of God's love you personally can be.

❖

"If you utter what is precious, and not what is worthless, you shall be as My mouth."
[JEREMIAH 15:19]

❖

Teach me, O gentle Lord, how to disagree without becoming disagreeable.

Little Boy Gives All to Clothing Drive

A 5-year-old boy decided to do something about it when he heard his kindergarten teacher tell of a clothing collection for poor children overseas.

The next morning, when his mother looked in his closet, she found that all the boy's clothes were missing.

A quick investigation by the startled mother revealed the cause—the youngster had taken every bit of his clothing to school.

Impetuous generosity is often a strong trait in young children. Such impulses need more to be strengthened and directed than squelched.

In a world where the expectations of the poor far outrun their advances, a growing number of competent, dedicated persons is required to help the rest of humanity to help themselves.

Each of us, by God's grace, has a part to play. The divinely rooted impulse to share with the needy can do much to overcome man's age-old foes of hunger, ignorance, disease and unbelief.

❖

"Do not neglect to do good and to share what you have, for such sacrifices are pleasing to God." [HEBREWS 13:16]

❖

Help me, heavenly Father, to apply the Gospel truths to modern life.

Fog Becomes a Best Seller

A booming business in selling "genuine London fog" was done by 2 American girls in England.

It wasn't long before the enterprising lassies, who were working as recreational supervisors, had sold 8,000 cans of fog at 35 cents each. Most of the buyers were U.S. citizens on their way home.

What prompted them to get into their off-beat side line was the fact that they received a package of fresh air from friends in Wisconsin. If you can send fresh air from Wisconsin, they asked, why not send London fog to America?

It is truly amazing what can be accomplished once the desire to sell is there.

Those who strenuously exert themselves either for personal profit or for less worthy reasons often outshine those who have a higher product to sell.

Use your own God-given powers of persuasion not just for self, but to protect the rights of the misunderstood, excluded and forgotten. You will thus bring the love and truth of Christ to a needy world.

❖

"Every one who acknowledges Me before men, I also will acknowledge before My Father who is in heaven." [MATTHEW 10:32]

❖

Never let me be content, O Lord, to do anything for You halfheartedly when I can do it wholeheartedly.

336

A Blind Man Teaches the Blind

A blind X-ray technician is teaching other sightless persons how they can lead constructive lives.

He began a four-week training program to help blind men and women learn a useful occupation in X-ray processing.

The blind instructor's philosophy is well summed up by one young person who said:

"I don't want to have a job because someone feels sorry for the poor little blind boy. I want to feel I have a job I can do."

One of the most hopeful signs in the world is the latent desire in every human being to make a personal contribution to life rather than be overly dependent on others.

It may be true that many lazily evade this divine instinct, which God has made a part of their very nature.

But they know in their hearts they can lead more complete and satisfying lives if they "put in" as well as "take out" of life.

✧

"Did I not tell you that if you would believe you would see the glory of God?" [JOHN 11:40]

✧

Thanks to You, O Creator, for the blessing of sight. Let me always use it properly.

Better Sleep for Cows

Cows are among the more contented customers of a mattress factory in Scotland.

The plant is turning out hundreds of foam-rubber mattresses each week for farmers who want their dairy herds to enjoy a good night's sleep. The results were described by a factory representative:

"During tests at several modern farms, we proved that the milk yield was considerably higher after the mattresses were installed," he said. "The reason is probably that the animal is more comfortable while asleep."

Modern improvements make it possible for man as well as animals to conserve energy. But care should be taken to see that this advantage is put to worthwhile use, not dissipated in a frivolous manner.

Seek ways and means of promoting the spiritual and material interests of the public. You will thereby be preparing yourself for a good night's sleep with that indispensable asset —a clear conscience.

✦

"In peace I will lie down and sleep; for You alone, O Lord, make me dwell in safety."

[PSALM 4:8]

✦

Let me spend and be spent, O Lord, in Your holy cause.

Thanks to One Woman

Thanksgiving became a national holiday mainly through the tireless efforts of one woman, Sarah Hale. For 17 years she carried on a single-handed campaign through talks, letters and magazine articles.

Despite widespread indifference, she kept at it, emphasizing the advantages that would result from a public expression of gratitude to God on a specific day for the whole country instead of at different times in the various states.

Impressed by Sarah Hale's tireless efforts, President Lincoln proclaimed November 26, 1863, to be a national day of Thanksgiving.

"It has seemed to me," he said, "fit and proper that God's blessings should be solemnly, reverently and gratefully acknowledged, as with one heart and one voice, by the whole American people."

Every year since then a special day has been set aside on which the American people formally give thanks for God's benefits.

✧

"Then we Your people . . . will give thanks to You for ever; from generation to generation we will recount Your praise." [PSALM 79:13]

✧

Thanks to You, O bountiful Father, for Your countless blessings to all men.

Boy Breaks Date with Dentist

Fancy footwork by a youngster who cut loose from a dentist's chair enabled him to put off the inevitable till another day.

With the bib still fastened around his neck, the 10-year-old boy ran out of the office in Gastonia, N.C. determined to avoid having a tooth pulled.

After he shot into the woods, a search party was organized to find him. It took 2½ hours before he was found, still wearing the bib, and brought home by his father.

Many of us get the urge to "head into the woods" when necessary but painful duties confront us. To feel this way is no more than human.

But little constructive and needed work would be done if all heeded the urge to put natural inclination ahead of the rigorous but rewarding summons of conscience.

Keep alive the divine spark by paying greater attention to the good that can be accomplished by your efforts to serve others than to the inconvenience it may cause you.

❖

"Through many tribulations we must enter the kingdom of God."   [ACTS 14:22]

❖

Hold me to my duties, O Lord, when everything around me forms an inducement to take the easy way out.

They Stuck to Their Jobs

Two men—one, an electrician for 67 years and the other, a window-washer for 45—have proven that they know how to stick to a job.

The electrician, a small white-haired man of 84, passed something of a milestone when he supervised the re-wiring of a building he had originally wired in 1906.

The window-washer, a spry 66, opens, washes and wipes an estimated 22,800 windows a year in Manhattan's Rockefeller Center.

Perseverance at a single occupation is not necessarily a virtue, but flitting about from one job to another is surely a defect.

If you know anyone who is doing a good job in any capacity that affects the material or spiritual well-being of men, you can perform a Christlike service by encouraging such a person to stay at his post.

By helping others to persevere, you do much to ensure your own perseverance.

✧

*"Be steadfast, immovable, always abounding
in the work of the Lord, knowing that in the
Lord your labor is not in vain."*
[1 CORINTHIANS 15:58]

✧

Grant me the strength, O Jesus, to work for
the benefit of others, in spite of any difficulties.

Errant Dart Leaves a Train of Trouble

A badly-aimed dart exploded an electric bulb in a London club, short-circuited the lights and plunged the room into darkness. But that was only the start.

While the dart-thrower muttered about his bad luck, the club's proprietor went down to the cellar to replace the fuse. He tripped on the stairs and was bitten by his own dog as he struggled to rise.

Meanwhile, another man cut his hand on a broken glass. To crown it all, somebody walked off with the dartboard.

"I haven't had an evening like this in all my 14 years here," exclaimed the bewildered owner.

Small mishaps have a way of triggering chain reactions that are not even faintly amusing.

The neglect of person after person to vote, to attend meetings or to take an honest stand can snowball into calamities in which everybody suffers.

Likewise, the smallest act for the love of God and others can start a trend for the better. The stakes are too high in today's world to trifle with danger.

❖

"If one member suffers, all suffer together."
[1 CORINTHIANS 12:26]

❖

Keep me ever mindful, O Lord, that even my least deeds will have consequences for time and eternity.

Postman Pays Tribute to Patrons

A rural mail carrier in Kentucky gave a happy surprise to all the families on his route when he retired recently. He sent each of them this postcard:

"Dear Patron: It has been a wonderful experience to serve such a fine and loyal group of people.

"I have rejoiced with many of you when you received letters from loved ones away from home. I have sorrowed when some received letters of bad news. I have anticipated with you that long-awaited letter that never came. When I made mistakes your understanding carried me on. May the years ahead bring you and your families much joy and peace."

You too can enrich the lives of countless others by showing a friendly concern for their best interests.

Seek every opportunity to be of service to others. Start at home and then reach out to the world with the Christlike determination to treat others as you yourself wish to be treated. Then you are bound to leave the world better than you found it.

✧

"I have given you an example, that you also should do as I have done to you."

[JOHN 13:15]

✧

Inspire me, O Holy Spirit, to bring joy and happiness into the lives of others.

Elderly Woman Saves Man's Life

A small, 85-year-old woman clutched a 250-pound man as he dangled upside down from the 6th floor window of her apartment.

The superintendent of the house was applying putty to the kitchen window when suddenly the metal guard rail snapped. The huge man fell backwards but kept his feet hooked on the window sill.

With one hand he grasped a piece of the railing fastened to the outside brick wall.

The elderly woman—only 5 feet tall—dropped her morning tea and rushed over to the open window. She held the man's feet for 10 minutes until neighbors and police heard their cries for help and pulled the big man back inside.

Unusual as such a case may be, it shows what can be done, with God's help, in spite of limitations.

Even if handicaps of one sort or another prevent you from doing everything you'd like to help your neighbor, you can do at least something.

If you won't, who will?

✣

"I can do all things in Him Who strengthens me." [PHILIPPIANS 4:13]

✣

Give me the inspiration, O Lord, to be ready with the effort needed when the love of neighbor calls for it.

Woodsman Knits Sweaters in Spare Time

A rugged Missouri woodsman has a unique hobby—knitting sweaters for friends and relatives.

The outdoorsman, who is employed by the department of forestry, spends his working hours cutting down or trimming trees. Much of his spare time is devoted to rock-hunting expeditions or stalking deer with bow and arrow.

But he is also the only male member of the advanced knitting class in the Adult Education program in University City, Missouri.

"I never did like to just sit around not doing anything," the 47-year-old bachelor explained, "so about 3 years ago, I bought a knitting book and just started following the directions. Since then I've made over 30 sweaters."

Most human beings soon tire of being idle. God instills in every person a divine urge to be creative and constructive—to do something to benefit others as well as themselves. The more free time you have, the greater effort you should make in behalf of the common good.

❖

"There are varieties of working, but it is the same God Who inspires them all in every one." [1 CORINTHIANS 12:6]

❖

Let me use well, O Master, whatever talent You have entrusted to me.

More Than Words Needed

Peace and deadly weapons don't go together, one man found out upon being fined $300 plus $9 court costs by a magistrate in Chester, Pa.

Despite the defendant's protests concerning his peaceful intentions, police discovered that he was carrying a cat-o'-nine-tails, a loaded starter pistol with steel slivers in the barrel, a knife and a homemade brass knuckle.

"Carrying any of these things is against the law. I want you to know that and tell your friends," the judge said.

To that, the man said: "I don't have any friends."

The judge said he could certainly understand why and with that imposed the fine.

It is easy to talk peace and at the same time be a cause of strife at home, on the job, in an organization or in any other setting. Little is accomplished by those who don't back up peaceful words with peaceful actions. The Lord asks each of us to be a "peacemaker" in fact as well as theory.

❖

"So far as it depends upon you, live peaceably with all." [ROMANS 12:18]

❖

Allow me to be an instrument of Your peace, O Lord.

Wisdom—Always in Short Supply

All men praise wisdom, though few possess it.

Closer investigation, however, may be helpful to anyone who wants to be wise in thought and action.

"Wisdom" is defined as: "The power of discerning what is true and right; in the Bible, ready insight into the divine law, with obedience to such law."

Another dictionary adds this: "In its full sense, wisdom implies the highest and noblest exercise of all the faculties of the moral nature as well as of the intellect."

One may have knowledge and be proud. Wisdom is humble.

One may have humility and be ill-informed. Wisdom is enlightened.

One may have enlightenment and be apathetic. Wisdom is active.

One may be active and misdirected. Wisdom thinks things through.

In the final analysis, wisdom is the gift by which man shares in the knowledge and love of God Himself.

✧

"If any of you lacks wisdom, let him ask God, who gives to all men generously." [JAMES 1:5]

✧

Grant me the wisdom, Lord, to know what I don't know—and to act rightly on what I do know.

347

An Old Cup That Taught a Lesson

Somerset Maugham, the novelist, had a cup—old and cracked —that he acquired during his escape from France aboard a small cargo ship in 1940.

The ship was crowded, the weather hot and water was rationed. Pointing to the old cup, he would tell friends: "That was what held my daily allowance of water."

Then he added: "Whenever I feel myself getting a bit stuffy and inclined to take the comfortable places I stay in and the good food I eat for granted, I fill my cup at the tap and drink it—slowly. Brings me back to earth again in quite a hurry."

There is nothing like an occasional jolt to remind us that our abilities are loaned to us by God for the service of all humanity.

Whether you are a writer, an office worker, a homemaker, an executive, a farmer or anything else, the Lord sent you into the world to carry out a mission. You can better do this if you are not puffed up with excessive self-importance.

❖

"In the time of plenty think of the time of hunger." [SIRACH 18:25]

❖

Make me realize that everything I have comes from You, Lord, and let me share my blessings with others.

Proposal Wrapped up in a Bottle

A bottle washed up on a Sicilian shore contained, not a plea for help, but a proposal of marriage.

"I want to marry the girl who finds this letter," it said. "Please write to this address: Kuguk-Bazar Cadd—No. 46, Istanbul, Turkey."

The sender added this postscript: "If you are not a girl throw this bottle in the sea again." And the teenage boy who found it did just that.

Few proposals are so bizarre and indiscriminate as this. Nevertheless, the high rate of broken marriages is a serious reminder that:

1. Adequate preparation and instruction are essential for this lifelong vocation, founded by God Himself.
2. Increasing emphasis is needed on the element of sacrifice and mutual self-giving unto death.
3. Parenthood is filled with awesome responsibilities as well as marvelous privileges.
4. The future of the nation and world depends, under God, on the climate of the home.

✤

"Let each one of you love his wife as himself, and let the wife see that she respects her husband." [EPHESIANS 5:33]

✤

Give me a profound appreciation for the holiness of marriage, O Lord, and help me share it with others.

Organizations Need Personal Interest

Work in any group can become quite cold and impersonal unless people go out of their way to inject a warm, personal note into everything they do.

Consider basic tips like these:

1. Be cordial instead of distant or hostile.
2. Blend gentleness with firmness when you must take a stand.
3. Keep lines of communication open.
4. Disagree without becoming disagreeable.
5. Give tactful assurance to those who are frustrated.
6. Respect the feelings and viewpoints of others, no matter how much you may differ.
7. Listen attentively when others have the floor. Whispering or causing distractions is discourteous, to say the least.

Countless opportunities exist to let God's love find its way into your words and actions . . . if you watch for them.

✧

"May the Lord make you increase and abound in love to one another and to all men."
[1 THESSALONIANS 3:12]

✧

Let me be a cooperator in worthwhile endeavors, O Lord, not a critic or complainer.

Carrier Pigeons Solve a Problem

A garage owner in Ware, England, found an unusual way to give wings to his words.

He became understandably impatient at news that he would have to wait until another 12 months before his telephone would be installed. So he decided to resort to carrier pigeons as a temporary means of communication.

The chief use of the birds, he explained, was to maintain contact between his present filling station and a new one he owns 5 miles away.

In these days of electronic transmission and fast travel, a carrier pigeon hardly seems to be much of a boon to communication. But circumstances can force one to resort to more elementary methods.

How quickly we communicate is often vital. But what we say and how we say it count even more.

Whether you share your ideas with others by carrier pigeon, telephone or face-to-face, do it truthfully, fairly and in a spirit of Christlike love.

Then your message will "get through," even if it takes a bit longer.

✧

"Rather, speaking the truth in love, we are to grow up in every way." [EPHESIANS 4:15]

✧

Teach me, O Father, to think, speak and act as You expect me to do.

351

Gratitude Expressed in Action

The generous spirit in which inmates of a Texas prison gave blood to 2 critically ill children has resulted in an employment program for men on parole.

It all began when prisoners in the Huntsville Penitentiary volunteered to give blood to 2 children with a severe anemic condition.

When one of the children died several months later, the inmates set up a permanent foundation to supply her surviving brother with all the transfusions he would need.

The father of the children, who worked for the Texas Employment Committee, was so deeply touched by their consideration that he enlisted the services of his superiors and fellow workers to find jobs for parolees who needed work. In less than a year, positions were found for 108 former convicts.

Gratitude that finds expression in specific action for others is close to the heart of Christ. In your own life try to say "thanks" by some constructive action however small.

✧

"Give thanks in all circumstances."
[1 THESSALONIANS 5:18]

✧

Let my gratitude ever overflow, O heavenly Father, with deeds that benefit my fellow human beings.

Youth Fixes Steeple Clock

A resourceful teenager made a $1,000 repair on a steeple clock for 25¢. The clock in the tower of a Milford, Connecticut, church had been silent for over a decade because of the high cost of fixing it.

The boy, a church member, decided to see if he could repair the 117-year-old clock himself.

"I just climbed into the steeple with a pair of pliers, an oil can and a few other tools," he said.

Spending only a quarter for parts, the youth soon had the old clock striking again after its long silence.

There are few thrills in life comparable to that experienced by persons whose actions disprove the skeptical opinion: "It can't be done."

True enough, many things cannot be accomplished at a given time because of circumstances or human limitations. But, with God's help, many others can, from improving communication in the family to making a positive contribution to political life. You'll never know until you try.

✧

"Let no one despise your youth, but set the believers an example in speech and conduct, in love, in faith, in purity."
[1 TIMOTHY 4:12]

✧

Give me determination to keep my sights high, Lord, and perseverance to see things through.

Overcome Your Worries

One doctor gave this admonition to persons tempted to side-step difficult situations:

"Don't push your worries behind your back where they can heckle you . . .

"Bring them out in front of you, line them up, and look them over . . .

"Decide which ones you can do something about and which ones you will have to live with . . .

"Don't waste your energies on things you can't change, but go into action on those you can."

It is difficult for most of us to say: "This is my problem." But it is the all-important first step.

Problems confronted are problems partly solved. Those we close our eyes to . . . whether personal, family, business, community or national . . . may be the very ones that come back to plague us in the long run.

The Lord expects us . . . and will assist us . . . to face up to problems of all types. If we do our part, He will surely do His.

✧

"Cast all your anxieties on Him, for He cares about you." [1 PETER 5:7]

✧

Aid me, Holy Spirit, to contribute to solutions rather than become part of the problem myself.

Teenage Journalist Retires

A lad who was probably the world's youngest editor-publisher retired recently at the age of 15.

When the Canadian teenager closed down his weekly newspaper, *The News Review*, he explained to his 180 subscribers, in 10 provinces, that he simply needed more time for his studies.

Regular readers who paid $3.50 a year for the mimeographed paper included the Prime Minister and the Leader of the Opposition, as well as the Chief Justice of Nova Scotia and the Premier of Newfoundland.

Besides printing the top news stories of the week, *The News Review* featured editorials, sports, riddles and a book section.

Such an early career is rather unusual. Nevertheless, parents and teachers who see writing ability in young people are in a unique position to encourage them to develop this God-given talent for the benefit of all.

Writers with competence and high motivation are needed in ever greater numbers.

✧

"With upright heart he tended them, and guided them with skillful hand."

[PSALM 78:72]

✧

Grant me the privilege, O Lord, of guiding at least one person into a writing career during my lifetime.

Boy Genius Dropped from College

After 6 weeks in college, a 12-year-old genius has been sent back to grade school in Florida.

It was not lack of brilliance for Billy has finished fifth out of a class of 30 at college, in a course dealing with the principles of energy, force and motion, meteorology and chemistry.

College officials were impressed by the boy's unique talent. But they also recognized that he was hampered in his attempts to solve physics and chemistry problems because he had skipped the fundamental training in high school mathematics.

Billy's parents said they were proud of his success in college, but admitted they were just as happy to have him return to "normalcy."

Most of us are not troubled by an overabundance of talent, but still we may fail to take the time and trouble to develop the well-rounded personality that God expects each of us to enjoy.

Show perseverance in bringing to full flower your intellectual, emotional and spiritual capabilities.

✧

"Each has his own special gift from God, one of one kind and one of another."

[1 CORINTHIANS 7:7]

✧

May I use well the talent You have entrusted to me, O divine Master.

356

Grateful Orphan Becomes Foster Mother

A woman who grew up in a foster home has helped dozens of homeless children since her marriage.

The Rockford, Ill., mother of four and her husband, a truck driver, have taken 48 foster babies into their home over the past five years.

"I was an orphan and I lived in a foster home for 12 years," she explained. "I always felt that if I could help little ones along the way I would try."

The babies, usually two or three of them at a time, come from the Children's Home of Rockford, and are cared for from birth until they are six or seven weeks old.

"Sure, it takes quite a bit of time," admits the foster mother. "And you can't take foster babies and not make sacrifices. But it's worth it."

Caring for children of any age is more of an effort than anyone but a parent would think possible.

For this reason, God must be especially pleased by parents who reach beyond their own homes to bring in other children who might not otherwise have the love and attention they so keenly need.

✧

"Whoever receives one such child in My name receives Me."   [MARK 9:37]

✧

Help me understand the problems of home life, Lord, and strengthen the unity of even one family.

Error Gladdens Turkish Farmer

A misplaced comma spelled good fortune for a Turkish farmer.

The man appeared briefly in a Danish television documentary filmed in Turkey, and the Denmark Radio Corporation sent him a check for his cooperation. The accounts department moved a comma to the right, and the amazed man received 10,000 Turkish pounds ($1,000)—ten times the amount he was owed.

The error was found when the worker sent the corporation a grateful letter, saying he had used the money to buy a farm near his village.

The company decided not to sue for the money's return. "We are happy it went to a needy person," a spokesman commented.

While there is reason to rejoice that a deserving person reaped a benefit, such cases are rare enough to make headlines.

By helping others find meaningful employment, we can be the Lord's instrument of peace and justice in an economically unbalanced world.

❖

"Open wide your hand to your brother, to the needy and to the poor in the land."
[DEUTERONOMY 15:11]

❖

Help me continue and even increase my efforts, Lord, to bring worthwhile values into life's mainstream.

Wanted: More Peacemakers

A sign hangs on the wall of one dedicated official who is often caught in the middle of various opposing groups.

It reads: "Blessed are the peacemakers—for they shall catch the devil from both sides!"

When misunderstandings, disputes and clashes arise, you can help clear the air by retaining your sense of humor.

During the dark days of the Civil War, Abraham Lincoln confided to a friend: "With the fearful strain that is on me night and day, if I did not laugh I should die."

The divine source of humor was aptly described by Thomas Carlyle in 1827: "True humor springs not more from the head than from the heart; it is not contempt, its essence is love."

You may not completely succeed. But you can at least reduce tensions and, with God's help, prevent the spread of strife.

✧

"Strive for peace with all men, and for the holiness without which no one will see the Lord."   [HEBREWS 12:14]

✧

Strengthen my resolve, O Father, to be a source of peace, not of dissension.

359

16 Days Without Sleep

By staying awake for 394 hours, a 51-year-old longshoreman in Finland claimed a world's record.

The determined man managed to get along without sleep for 16 days and 10 hours. He overcame every temptation to doze off by drinking fruit juice, taking long walks and rolling in the snow.

Once a man sets his heart on any objective, however difficult it may be, he will subject himself to the most severe self-discipline. He will endure personal hardships that he would otherwise regard as foolhardy, were it not that his ultimate aim is continually before him.

If we human beings would pursue eternal goals with the same drive and dedication that we devote to achieving worldly fame, ambition or self-satisfaction, we would soon become saints.

Set your sights on worthwhile goals both here and hereafter and you will be more apt to lead a happy, balanced and meaningful life.

✧

"But seek first His kingdom and His right-eousness, and all these things shall be yours as well." [MATTHEW 6:33]

✧

May I show the same concern for the needs of others, O Lord, that I devote to my own whims.

Youth Leads to Solving of Age-Old Puzzle

How the ninth century Vikings could navigate so accurately, even when sun and stars were obscured by clouds, has long puzzled scientists. It took a 10-year-old Danish boy to find the answer.

The youth got his idea after he read a magazine article describing the so-called "sun stones" used by the early Viking sailors.

To him they sounded very much like the twilight compass. This device has a Polaroid filter that enables pilots to find the sun on cloudy days in latitudes where the magnetic compass is unreliable.

The boy's father contacted the author of the article, who searched until he found a transparent crystal called cordierite, which turns from yellow to dark blue when held at a certain angle to the sun. With such a "sun stone," the ancient mariners could have navigated with considerable accuracy.

Youth can have insight overlooked by their more preoccupied elders. They are a gift of God, and as such are to be nourished and respected.

✧

"There are varieties of gifts, but the same Spirit." [1 CORINTHIANS 12:4]

✧

Never let me close my mind, Holy Spirit, to new ideas, whether they come from young or old.

Girl, 12, Masterminds Robberies

A ring of child burglars who broke into a home in a New York suburb and stole money for thrills was masterminded by a 12-year-old girl.

The youngsters, all from well-to-do homes and ranging in age from 12 to 15, were picked up by police in the midst of their thieving expeditions.

The girl leader, police said, plotted robberies like a professional. She telephoned residences to see if anyone was home before sending her accomplices into action.

All told, the children burglarized 21 homes, walking in through an unlocked door or by smashing a window to gain entry. They were responsible for about $500 worth of thefts and damage.

The tendency of young people to drift into mischief is often motivated more by a hankering to be "up and doing" than by a desire to be downright malicious.

Discover and harness the energy and enterprise that the good Lord entrusts to each young person and you will do a service to everyone.

✧

"Make them know the way in which they must walk and what they must do."
[EXODUS 18:20]

✧

Instill in boys and girls, O divine Master, a determination to build up rather than to tear down.

362

Post Office Can't Give Money Away

The inability to give back $8 million is plaguing the Chicago Post Office.

This unusual problem followed the government's decision to discontinue the postal savings system.

However, despite notices to those who had accounts, a postal spokesman announced: "Some 42,000 depositors have made no effort to remove their money from the main post office and its branches."

A partial explanation may be that many of the depositors, especially the smaller ones, have died and postal officials have never been notified.

When H. G. Bohn said in 1855 that "Money is a good servant but a bad master," he was uttering a truth known to all.

It is often difficult to tell whether our possessions serve or master us. One test is the way in which we use them as a gift of God for the relief of others as well as for the benefit of self and family.

We should all try to steer a middle course between being a tightwad and a spendthrift.

✧

"If riches increase, set not your heart on them." [PSALM 62:10]

✧

Make me conscious, Lord, of the proper use of every possession that You have loaned to me.

Adrift on a Cake of Ice

Two hungry, frostbitten Eskimos were rescued from a floating block of ice near Alaska, after it had broken off an ice pack in the Bering Sea last winter and drifted 150 miles south.

A United States Air Force helicopter sighted the stranded men and plucked them off the moving ice.

While few persons will ever find themselves in such a predicament, there are times when one feels cut off from everybody and everything, drifting aimlessly and helplessly towards nowhere.

There is a natural temptation to lapse into despair under such disheartening circumstances. But easy as it is to give in to gloomy pessimism, it is important to remember that hopelessness only makes a bad situation even worse. It cripples initiative and discourages a person from even trying.

No matter how desperate things may seem, make sure you do not guarantee defeat by becoming completely cynical. Keep hoping, praying and trying for a solution, and you will at least have done your best.

❖

"Rejoice in your hope, be patient in tribulation, be constant in prayer." [ROMANS 12:12]

❖

Be to me a hope in the midst of discouragement, O Lord.

Why You Should Be Cheerful

To be cheerful amid all circumstances is not easy. These reminders may help you to be a source of joy and gladness rather than a spreader of gloom:

1. "The plainest sign of wisdom is a continual cheerfulness." (MICHEL DE MONTAIGNE, 1580)
2. "A light heart lives long." (SHAKESPEARE, 1595)
3. "Cheerfulness keeps up a kind of daylight in the mind." (JOSEPH ADDISON, 1712)
4. "Wondrous is the strength of cheerfulness and its power of endurance. The cheerful man will do more in the same time, will do it better, will persevere in it longer, than the sad or sullen." (THOMAS CARLYLE, 1840)
5. "We ought to be as cheerful as we can, if only because to be happy ourselves is a most effectual contribution to the happiness of others." (JOHN LUBBOCK, 1890)

Think of yourself as an instrument of the Lord in bringing His divine gaiety into the lives of those who are depressed or antagonistic and you will be more apt to persevere in your efforts to be habitually cheerful.

✧

"Be of good cheer, I have overcome the world." [JOHN 16:33]

✧

Help me, O Holy Spirit, to be cheerful when I tend to be indifferent or dejected.

Finds Diamonds on Subway Train

A diamond salesman who lost $22,000 worth of gems on a New York subway found that "there are still honest people around."

When the salesman left the train, a Brooklyn student noticed that he had left one of his cases behind. He shouted at the man, but it was too late.

The student, who was working his way through college as a taxi driver, turned in the case of diamonds to the Transit Authority's "lost and found" department. Officials located the salesman.

"It's just nice to know that there are still honest people around," the relieved man commented. His next move was to meet the student, who, he said, will be rewarded for his honesty.

The capacity to be truthful and honest has been instilled in every person by the Creator. No matter how much or how often people slip into dishonorable ways, there is always great hope that within each individual is the power to be trustworthy.

✧

"For the Lord is righteous, He loves righteous deeds; the upright shall behold His face."
[PSALM 11:7]

✧

Keep me conscious, O Father, that I am always in Your presence.

The Best Gift of All

All of a 9-year-old California boy's presents last Christmas were lost in a fire—except one.

He told firemen in Redwood City, California: "I saved the best gift of all—my mother's life."

The 43-year-old woman was taken to the hospital for treatment of burns over 25 per cent of her body. But she was alive, thanks to the efforts of her son. She had been asleep on a couch in the living room when the fire started and, with the help of firemen, the youngster beat out the flames in her clothes. Then he hurried to awaken his two brothers.

Children who learn to love their parents do themselves a great service. They bring out latent qualities that otherwise might never be developed.

In generously fulfilling the divine command: "Thou shalt honor thy parents," young people live up to their best instincts.

They likewise avoid the personal loss incurred by all who show a lack of love and devotion to their fathers and mothers.

✧

"Honor your father and mother."
[EPHESIANS 6:2]

✧

Teach us, O Father, to show our parents the respect and honor that they, as Your representatives, deserve.

"Wonderful Blessing" through Small Boy

A 13-year-old boy gave a blind woman a Christmas present that she will never forget.

When the teenager, who worked afternoons for a Memphis, Tennessee, pharmacy, went to the tumble-down home of a 71-year-old blind woman to deliver medicine, he was shocked at the poverty he saw there.

Talking with the woman, he learned that she had not had a Christmas tree for many years. Just before the holiday the 7th grade youngster brought a tree to the old woman's house, set it up and trimmed it with lights, decorations and gifts.

The aged woman was delighted. "I can feel it and smell it all over the house," she said. "The Lord has sent me a wonderful blessing through this child."

With a little imagination, each of us can find needs in the lives of others that we can fill, in our individual way, with God's blessings.

If you remember that you can be an instrument of God's love, you will be alert to the countless opportunities of bringing joy into the life of every person you meet.

❖

"This is My commandment, that you love one another as I have loved you."   [JOHN 15:12]

❖

May I seek to put love where there is no love,
O Holy Spirit.

A Handful of Shepherds

A few "nobodies" were singled out by almighty God on the first Christmas to represent all mankind in paying homage to the new-born Savior—and to be first to announce the "good news" to others.

They were unlettered shepherds, rough-and-ready men, who lived on the fringe of civilization. But the small efforts they made have been an inspiration to millions down through the centuries.

Reflect on the Gospel account of these poor shepherds, as told in chapter two of St. Luke:

> They were the first to be told—"The angel said to them, 'Be not afraid; for behold, I bring you good news of a great joy which will come to all the people; for to you is born this day in the city of David a Savior, who is Christ the Lord.' " [10,11]
> They responded immediately—"They went with haste, and found Mary and Joseph, and the Babe lying in a manger." [16]
> They didn't keep it to themselves—"And all who heard it wondered at what the shepherds told them." [18]

In God's sight, no one is a "nobody." Each has an eternal value for what he is and does.

✧

> Grant me, O Lord, the grace of knowing my importance in Your sight and the mission You want me to accomplish.

Dad Has Mishap at Delivery Room

One expectant father will never forget the birth of his second child in a Phoenix, Ariz., hospital.

The man suffered multiple fractures of the jaw when he slipped and fell at the door of the delivery room.

"I got dizzy looking in the room," he later explained. "I'll be on a baby diet for a day or two, eating the same kind of food the baby will eat."

Meanwhile, the mother and child were reported in good condition.

Undue apprehension can trigger adverse reactions. Sometimes those events over which we had the most concern may be worsened, instead of helped, by worry. The unexpected is not as unlikely as it may seem.

Try to see in every occurrence, therefore, a God-given opportunity. He will supply you the strength.

Then you will be less apprehensive and more likely to keep emotion under the control of reason and will.

Doing this is no guarantee that life will be any less full of surprises, but it should enable you to accept surprises more effectively.

✧

"Which of you by being anxious can add one cubit to his span of life?" [MATTHEW 6:27]

✧

Keep me from letting down my guard, O Holy Spirit, so that I may be ready for whatever You have in store.

370

A Conductor with a Heart

Absent-minded commuters who are fortunate enough to board one suburban train without their wallets find a sympathetic friend in the conductor.

He not only lets them pay their fare to New York the next morning, but lends them $5 or $10 out of his own pocket to meet the day's other emergencies.

The New Haven Railroad trainman has been making these small loans for twenty years and says he has no regrets. Losses have been remarkably small—only $10 a year.

"I am more than repaid in kind notes from commuters," he said. "Sometimes they enclose an extra dollar or two which I turn over to one of my charities."

Make the most of every opportunity to help those in a predicament and you will enrich the lives of countless others as well as your own.

By showing a sympathetic interest in the troubles of others, especially those who do not know where to turn in their distress, you are imitating the Redeemer Himself.

❖

"That the love with which you have loved Me may be in them and I in them." [JOHN 17:26]

❖

Open my eyes, O Holy Spirit, to the innumerable opportunities to be of service to others.

Work Now, Rest Later

The "athletic phenomenon of all times" was the tribute paid to the late golf champion, Babe Didrickson Zaharias.

But few persons realize what hard labor went into making her success possible. While she was often referred to as "an automatic champion, a natural athlete," in reality she labored hard each and every day to perfect her golf game.

One person who knew her well said: "She hit as many as 1,000 balls in one afternoon, playing until her hands were so sore they had to be taped."

Work—hard work—is the price most people have to pay for success, be it material, mental or spiritual.

In fact, there is hardly any realistic goal we cannot reach with proper motivation and diligence.

Instead of following the line of least resistance and avoiding purposeful work, keep ever in mind that God intended man to labor. Reap blessings in both this life and the next by constant work and prayers.

✧

"I will give to each of you as your works deserve."　　　[REVELATION 2:23]

✧

Teach me to put into life as well as take out, O Lord.

One-Woman Attack on Poverty

With paperback books instead of bullets, one woman is waging a single-handed war on poverty.

It began when Mrs. Ben Benjamin of Los Angeles, with her husband's encouragement, decided to do more than complain about slum conditions.

So she contacted the principal of a school in the Watts area and offered him a check that provided him with funds to buy over 100 books for his students.

With the help of friends and school officials, sparked by her initiative, the number of books contributed to depressed area schools exceeds 7,000.

"Those children can't get out of the ghetto now," she said, "but they can sure read themselves out. Once they learn reading is a pleasure they'll be motivated to learn."

Such a program could be duplicated everywhere there is need—if enough people care. The Lord gives countless opportunities for us to share His blessings with others. But He expects us, as a "committee-of-one," to take the necessary first steps.

✧

"Put away violence and oppression, and execute justice and righteousness."

[EZEKIEL 45:9]

✧

Enlighten me, Lord, to see where human need is great and spur me to do something to relieve it.

Cafeteria Has 100 Clocks

More than 100 clocks on the walls of a cafeteria in Charleston, West Virginia, tick, tock, strike and chime throughout the big dining room. Diners cannot fail to be well aware of the time of day.

All the timepieces belong to the owner of the cafeteria who has collected them over the years. He now owns more than 300 clocks. They range from a tiny "Black Forest" cuckoo to a seven-foot-tall grandfather clock with walnut case and porcelain face.

Dozens of them are at present stored in the basement of the cafeteria, waiting to be displayed after they have been repaired.

No matter how many clocks may remind us of the fact, it is still difficult to realize that the only time we are really sure of is the present.

If we remember that each tick of the clock brings us a step closer to eternity, we will add much meaning to all that we think, say and do. Follow the advice of Lord Chesterfield: "Take care of the minutes, for the hours will take care of themselves."

✧

*"In all you do, remember the end of your life,
and then you will never sin."* [SIRACH 7:36]

✧

Help me, Lord, to know the value of time and use it well.

All Journeys Must End

Life is a journey. But have you ever stopped to think of the word "journey"?

The dictionary defines it as "the passage from one place to another; period of travel, sometimes applied figuratively to the passage of life."

"Journey" comes from the French "*journee*" and has its roots in a Latin word meaning "day." The French greeting "*bonjour*" means "good day."

Any journey has a destination. It differs from a tour, in that a tour returns to its starting place, and from an excursion, which is taken for pleasure.

"Like pilgrims to th' appointed place we tend," said the English poet John Dryden (1631–1701). "The world's an inn, and death the journey's end."

In "Twelfth Night" Shakespeare made this significant comment: "Journeys end in lovers' meeting."

Yes, life's journey, long or short, has a destination. It is meant to end in the eternal meeting with the God Who created us and loves us. Travel light, then, and let the works of love accompany you.

✧

"For a thousand years in Your sight are but as yesterday when it is past, or as a watch in the night." [PSALM 90:4]

✧

Keep me ever aware, Lord, that every day brings me closer to endless happiness with You.